CANADIAN SOCCER HISTORY MEN'S AMATEUR FOOTBALL CHAMPIONS

CANADIAN SOCCER HISTORY: MEN'S AMATEUR FOOTBALL CHAMPIONS (1913 to 2023)

FOOTBALLMEDIA / BY RICHARD SCOTT
COPYRIGHT © 2024 UP NORTH PRODUCTIONS.
NO REPRODUCTION WITHOUT PERMISSION.
ALL RIGHTS RESERVED.

PUBLISHED IN CANADA BY:
UP NORTH PRODUCTIONS
1995 INDIAN CREEK ROAD
LIMOGES, ON   K0A 2M0
BOOKS@FOOTBALLMEDIA.CA

Cover designed by Griffin Scott.
Challenge Trophy image courtesy Canada Soccer.

This publication features collected records and results from more than 110 years of Canadian football. Lineups and details are sometimes missing. For corrections and updates, please email us at books@footballmedia.ca.

CANADIAN SOCCER HISTORY SERIES
With tribute to the Canadian football writers from yesteryear, from Colin Jose (Canada Soccer) to Jeff Cross (Vancouver), Roy Jukich (Vancouver), Dunc Scott (Calgary), Vince Leah (Winnipeg), Bill Entwistle (Toronto), Billy Fenton (Toronto), George Gross (Toronto), Ed Waring (Toronto), Doug Campbell (Montréal), Norman Gillespie (Montréal) and many, many more.

CANADIAN SOCCER HISTORY: MEN'S AMATEUR FOOTBALL CHAMPIONS (1913 to 2023)

CHAMPIONS OF CANADA	4
FIRST DECADE 1910s	7
1920s	13
1930s	25
1940s	37
1950s	43
1960s	55
1970s	65
1980s	77
1990s	89
2000s	101
2010s	113
THE NEW DECADE	125

● ● ●

■ CONNAUGHT CUP ■

CHAMPIONS OF CANADA (1913 to 2023)

LAST DAY of ROUND ROBIN	CONNAUGHT CUP WINNERS	RUNNERS UP
1913-09-06 Fort William, ON	Norwood Wanderers FC of St. Boniface	Lachine
1914-09-12 Winnipeg, MB	Norwood Wanderers FC of St. Boniface	Fort William CPR

LAST DAY of FINAL (2 LEGS)	CONNAUGHT CUP WINNERS	RUNNERS UP
1915-08-12 Toronto, ON	Winnipeg Scottish FC series 6-1	Toronto Lancashire FC
1919-08-16 Montréal, QC	Montréal Grand Trunk FC series 3-1	Winnipeg Great War Vets
1920-09-06 Toronto, ON	Hamilton Westinghouse FC series 2-1	Hamilton Brittania
1921-08-06 Toronto, ON	Toronto Scottish FC series 4-0	Ladysmith FC
1922-08-12 Toronto, ON	Calgary Hillhurst FC series 2-1	Toronto Ulster United FC
1923-08-08 Winnipeg, MB (3)	Nanaimo City FC series 2-1	Montréal CPR
1924-07-26 Winnipeg, MB	United Weston FC series 3-2	Beloeil Canadian Explosives
1925-07-29 Winnipeg, MB (3)	Toronto Ulster United FC series 3-1	Nanaimo City FC

LAST DAY of FINAL (2 LEGS)	CHALLENGE TROPHY WINNERS	RUNNERS UP
1926-08-04 Winnipeg, MB (4)	United Weston FC series 3-2	Cumberland FC
1927-08-03 Winnipeg, MB	Nanaimo City FC series 14-1	Fort William Legion

LAST DAY of FINAL (BEST OF 3)	CHALLENGE TROPHY WINNERS	RUNNERS UP
1928-08-01 Winnipeg, MB	Westminster Royals FC (W L W)	Montréal CNR
1929-07-31 Winnipeg, MB (2)	Montréal Canadian National Railway (W W)	United Weston FC
1930-08-02 Winnipeg, MB	Westminster Royals FC (W L W)	Montréal CNR
1931-08-03 Winnipeg, MB (2)	Westminster Royals FC (W W)	Toronto Scottish FC
1932-07-30 Toronto, ON (2)	Toronto Scottish FC (W W)	North Shore United FC
1933-08-07 Winnipeg, MB	Toronto Scottish FC (D D W)	Prince Albert City Reds
1934-08-16 Winnipeg, MB	Verdun Park FC (W L W)	Prince Albert City Reds
1935-08-24 Winnipeg, MB (4)	Montréal Aldred FC (W L D W)	Nanaimo City FC
1936-08-12 Vancouver, BC	Westminster Royals FC (W L W)	United Weston FC
1937-08-02 Winnipeg, MB	Vanc. Johnston National Storage FC (L W W)	Ulster United FC
1938-08-17 Winnipeg, MB (5)	North Shore United FC (D L W D W)	Timmins Dome Mines
1939-08-05 Winnipeg, MB (4)	Vancouver Radials FC (D L W W)	Montréal Carsteel FC
1946-08-29 Toronto, ON (2)	Toronto Ulster United FC (W W)	Fort William ANAF
1947-09-22 Vancouver, BC (2)	Vancouver St. Andrews FC (W W)	Winnipeg Scottish FC
1948-08-11 Toronto, ON	Montréal Carsteel FC (W L W)	Vancouver St. Andrews FC
1949-08-10 Calgary, AB	North Shore United FC (W L W)	Hamilton Westinghouse FC
1950-08-14 Vancouver, BC	Vancouver City FC (W W)	Winnipeg ANAF Scottish FC
1951-09-18 Montréal, QC	Toronto Ulster United FC (D W D)	Vancouver St. Andrews FC
1952-09-04 Winnipeg, MB	Montréal Stelco (L W W)	Westminster Royals FC
1953-08-18 Montréal, QC	Westminster Royals FC (D W D)	Montréal Hakoah FC
1954-08-29 Winnipeg, MB (2)	Winnipeg AN&AF Scottish FC (W W)	North Shore United FC
1955-09-21 Toronto, ON	New Westminster Royals FC (W D D)	SA Ukraina Montréal

CHAMPIONSHIP FINAL	CHALLENGE TROPHY WINNERS	RUNNERS UP
1956-09-15 Vancouver, BC	Vancouver Hale-Co FC won 5-1	Winnipeg FC Germania
1957-09-22 Montréal, QC	SA Ukraina Montréal won 2-1	North Shore United FC
1958-09-20 Vancouver, BC	Westminster Royals FC won 2-0	Winnipeg AN&AF Scottish FC
1959-09-20 Toronto, ON	Montréal Canadian Alouettes won 3-2	Westminster Royals FC
1960-10-23 Vancouver, BC	Westminster Royals FC won 4-0	SC Golden Mile Toronto
1961-07-29 Montréal, QC	Montréal Concordia FC won 1-0	Vancouver Firefighters FC
1962-09-22 Winnipeg, MB	Winnipeg AN&AF Scottish FC won 6-0	Edmonton Edelweiss
1964-09-19 Vancouver, BC	Vancouver Columbus FC won 4-0	Sudbury Italia FC
1965-09-25 Oshawa, ON	Vancouver Firefighters FC won 5-0	Oshawa Italia FC
1966-09-03 Winnipeg, MB	British Columbia Selects won 2-0	Équipe Québec
1967-09-30 Calgary, AB	Toronto Ballymena United FC won 1-0	Calgary Kickers FC
1968-09-29 Toronto, ON	Toronto Royals FC won 1-0	Vancouver Columbus FC

CHALLENGE TROPHY

CHAMPIONSHIP FINAL		CHALLENGE TROPHY WINNERS	RUNNERS UP
1969-09-28	Burnaby, BC	Vancouver Columbus FC won 10-0	SA Ukraina Montréal
1970-08-06	Winnipeg, MB	Manitoba Selects won 2-1	Équipe Québec
1971-10-03	Burnaby, BC	Eintracht SC Vancouver won 3-1	Windsor Maple Leafs
1972-10-01	Toronto, ON	Westminster Labatt's Blues won 3-0	Toronto San Fili SC
1973-09-03	St. John's, NL	Vancouver Firefighters FC won 2-0	West Indies United Toronto
1974-08-25	St. John's, NL	Calgary Springer Kickers won 2-1	Windsor SS Italia
1975-08-24	Calgary, AB	Victoria London Boxing AC won 3-1	St. Lawrence Laurentians
1976-08-29	Winnipeg, MB	Victoria West FC won 3-2	Winnipeg Fort Rouge
1977-09-11	St. Lawrence, NL	Vancouver Columbus FC won 1-0	St. Lawrence Laurentians
1978-09-10	Kitchener, ON	Vancouver Columbus FC won 3-1	Elio Blues de Montréal
1979-09-16	Victoria, BC	Victoria West FC won 6-2	LaSalle Olympique SC
1980-09-14	Halifax, NS	Saint John Islanders won 3-2	Ottawa Maple Leaf Almrausch
1981-10-11	Calgary, AB	North York Ciociaro SC won 2-1	Calgary Springer Kickers
1982-10-10	Saskatoon, SK	Victoria West FC won 4-0	Saskatoon United SC
1983-10-10	Thunder Bay, ON	Vancouver Firefighters FC won 2-1	CNSC Windsor Croatia
1984-10-07	Victoria, BC	Victoria West FC won 1-0	Hamilton Dundas United
1985-10-14	Edmonton, AB	Croatia SC Vancouver won 3-0	Elio Blues de Montréal
1986-10-13	Sherbrooke, QC	Hamilton Steelers won 1-0	Croatia SC Vancouver
1987-10-12	Winnipeg, MB	Winnipeg Lucania SC won 1-0	New Westminster QPR
1988-10-10	Saskatoon, SK	Holy Cross FC won 2-0	Edmonton Italia Canadians
1989-10-09	St. John's, NL	Scarborough Azzurri won 3-2	Holy Cross FC
1990-10-08	Dartmouth, NS	Vancouver Firefighters FC won 1-0 aet	Dartmouth United
1991-10-14	Saskatoon, SK	NorVan ANAF 2-2 / won 4-2 on kicks	Scarborough Azzurri
1992-10-12	Burnaby, BC	NorVan ANAF won 1-0	Edmonton Scottish SC
1993-10-11	Etobicoke, ON	Vancouver Westside FC won 1-0	Calommiers Longueuil
1994-10-10	Edmonton, AB	Edmonton Itali Canadians SC won 1-0	Scarborough Azzurri
1995-10-09	Winnipeg, MB	Mistral-Estrie won 1-0	Halifax King of Donair
1996-10-14	New Minas, NS	Vancouver Westside FC won 2-1	Cosmos LaSalle
1997-10-13	Calgary, AB	Edmonton Italia Canadians SC won 3-1	North Shore Pegasus
1998-10-12	Fredericton, NB	CS Rivière-des-Prairies won 1-0	Hamilton Serbian
1999-10-11	Chilliwack, BC	Calgary Celtic SFC won 1-0	Coquitlam Metro-Ford SC
2000-10-09	Saskatoon, SK	Winnipeg Lucania SC won 2-0	Vancouver Westside FC
2001-10-08	Vaughan, ON	Halifax King of Donair won 4-1	Victoria Gorge FC
2002-10-14	St. John's, NL	Winnipeg Sons of Italy won 1-0	St. Lawrence Laurentiens
2003-10-13	Québec, QC	Calgary Callies 1-1 / won 4-2 on kicks	Panellinios Montréal FC
2004-10-11	Charlottetown, PE	Surrey FC Pegasus 0-0 / won 4-3 on kicks	Ottawa Royals
2005-10-10	Calgary, AB	Scarborough GS United won 3-2 act	Edmonton Green & Gold
2006-10-09	Surroy, BC	Ottawa St. Anthony SC won 1-0	Calgary Callies
2007-10-08	Halifax, NS	Calgary Callies won 5-0	Vancouver Columbus FC
2008-10-13	St. John's, NL	Calgary Callies won 3-1	Corfinium St-Léonard
2009-10-12	Saskatoon, SK	Winnipeg Hellas FC won 1-0	Royal-Sélect Beauport
2010-10-11	Charlottetown, PE	Charlottetown Abbies SC won 2-0 aet	Victoria Gorge FC
2011-10-10	Brossard, QC	Saskatoon HUSA Alumni won 2-0	Surrey ICST Pegasus
2012-10-08	Winnipeg, MB	Royal-Sélect Beauport 3-3 / won 4-2 on kicks	Edm. Scottish
2013-10-14	Halifax, NS	Gloucester Celtic FC won 3-0	Surrey United Firefighters
2014-10-13	Vaughan, ON	London Marconi SC 0-0 / won 4-2 on kicks	Calgary Callies
2015-10-12	Calgary, AB	London Marconi SC won 2-1	Edmonton Scottish SC
2016-10-10	St. John's, NL	Edmonton Scottish SC won 1-0	Royal-Sélect Beauport
2017-10-09	Surrey, BC	Western Halifax FC won 1-0	FC Winnipeg Lions
2018-10-08	Saskatoon, SK	Surrey BC Tigers Hurricanes won 7-3	Caledon SC
2019-10-14	St. John's, NL	Surrey Central City Breakers won 2-0	Ottawa St. Anthony SC
2022-10-10	Vaughan, ON	Gloucester Celtic FC won 2-0	Edmonton Green & Gold
2023-10-09	Halifax, NS	West Ottawa SC won 1-0	Western Halifax FC

CANADIAN SOCCER HISTORY
MEN'S AMATEUR FOOTBALL CHAMPIONS

FIRST DECADE

1913 Norwood Wanderers FC
FIRST DOMINION CHAMPIONSHIP

1-6 SEPTEMBER 1913 - ARENA PARK IN FORT WILLIAM, ONTRAIO

Norwood won the first Connaught Cup

Norwood Wanderers FC won the inaugural Dominion of Canada Football Championship after they clinched first place across a six-day tournament in Fort William, Ontario. The Manitoba-based club went undefeated across three matches and they clinched the title with a 2-2 draw against the hosts Fort William CPR on the final day of the series. Newly-elected Dominion of Canada Football Association President Tom Watson presented the Connaught Cup to Norwood captain Alex Simpson.

Four clubs participated in the inaugural edition of the Connaught Cup Series represented by regional winners from Manitoba, Ontario, New Ontario and Québec.

Centre half Bill Innes was the hero of the 1913 Connaught Cup Series while Symonds was the top scorer with five goals in three matches. Billy Bradshaw was the other Norwood goalscorer in their opening match while goalkeeper Albert Shoobert posted the clean sheet in their only win of the tournament.

CHAMPIONS : NORWOOD WANDERERS FC

1913 Norwood Wanderers FC of St. Boniface : GK Albert Shoobert; Bill Anderson, Alex Simpson; Harry McMaster, Bill Innes, Bob Whitehead; Billy McFarlane, Billy Bradshaw, W. Symonds, Bob Cook, Boyd Mayson. Manager Fred Rogers, Trainer C. Rogers. Winners received their 1913 medals in April 1914.

MANITOBA SOCCER CUP	PROVINCIAL WINNERS	SCORE	RUNNERS UP
1913-08-22 Portage la Prairie, MB	Norwood Wanderers FC	W 7-2	L Minnedosa
CONNAUGHT CUP SERIES	**ROUND ROBIN SERIES**	**SCORE**	**OPPONENT**
1913-09-02 Fort William, ON	Norwood Wanderers FC	W 3-0	L Lachine
1913-09-03 Fort William, ON	Norwood Wanderers FC	D 1-1	D Toronto Old Country
1913-09-06 Fort William, ON	Norwood Wanderers FC	D 2-2	D Fort William CPR

STANDINGS : Norwood 4 points; Lachine 3 points; Fort William 3 points; Toronto 2 points. Norwood Wanderers FC's six goals were scored by W. Symonds (5) and Billy Bradshaw. Hero of the Connaught Cup Series : centre half Bill Innes.

Norwood Wanderers FC
SECOND DOMINION CHAMPIONSHIP

7-12 SEPTEMBER 1914 - WINNIPEG ARENA IN MANITOBA

Norwood repeated as Cup champions

Norwood Wanderers FC captured their second-consecutive Dominion of Canada Football Championship after they clinched first place in a round-robin series at Winnipeg. Norwood won the series on the last day after a 1-0 win over Lachine. Both Norwood Wanderers FC and Fort William CPR were tied on six points, but Norwood finished first with a better goals average across four undefeated matches.

Norwood scored four goals and conceded just one while Fort William scored eight goals and conceded three. Norwood goalkeeper Walter Simpson posted three clean sheets.

Five clubs participated in the second Dominion of Canada Football Championship represented by regional winners from Saskatchewan, Manitoba, Ontario, New Ontario and Québec. Upon winning the Connaught Cup, the Norwood Wanderers were celebrated along a motorcar parade from Winnipeg to St. Boniface City Hall where they were congratulated by Mayor Fortunat Lachance.

CHAMPIONS : NORWOOD WANDERERS FC
1914 Norwood Wanderers FC of St. Boniface : GK Walter Simpson; Harry Ambler, Baird, Billy Bradshaw, Grant, Jackson, McDowell, Harry McMaster, McRae, Nicholson, Patterson, Albert Shoobert, Alex Simpson, Steele, Wakeley.

MANITOBA SOCCER CUP	PROVINCIAL WINNERS	SCORE	RUNNERS UP
1914-08-29 Winnipeg, MB	Norwood Wanderers FC D	? D	Winnipeg Scottish FC
1914-08-31 Winnipeg, MB	Norwood Wanderers FC D	? D	Winnipeg Scottish FC
1941-09-01 Winnipeg, MB	Norwood Wanderers FC W	1-0 L	Winnipeg Scottish FC
CONNAUGHT CUP SERIES	**ROUND ROBIN SERIES**	**SCORE**	**OPPONENT**
1914-09-07 Winnipeg, MB	Norwood Wanderers FC D	0-0 D	Toronto Eaton FC
1914-09-08 Winnipeg, MB	Norwood Wanderers FC D	1-1 D	Fort William CPR
1914-09-10 Winnipeg, MB	Norwood Wanderers FC W	2-0 L	Regina Leader
1914-09-12 Winnipeg, MB	Norwood Wanderers FC W	1-0 L	Lachine

STANDINGS : Norwood 6 points; Fort William 6 pts; Toronto 5 pts; Lachine 3 pts; Regina 0 pts. Norwood Wanderers FC's four goals scored by Jackson, Wakeley, McRae and Nicholson. Hero of the Connaught Cup Series : goalkeeper Walter Simpson.

■ CONNAUGHT CUP ■

1915 *Winnipeg Scottish FC*
FIRST DOMINION CHAMPIONSHIP

11-12 AUGUST 1915 - VARSITY STADIUM IN TORONTO, ONTARIO

Winnipeg won Cup on six-goal outburst

Winnipeg Scottish FC won the Connaught Cup after they exploded for six goals against Toronto Lancashire FC in the second leg of the 1915 Dominion of Canada Football Championship. Winnipeg won the two-leg Final 6-1 on aggregate after a 0-0 draw and a 6-1 win on back-to-back nights at Toronto's Varsity Stadium. Dominion of Canada Football Association President Craig Campbell presented the Connaught Cup to Winnipeg vice-captain Billy Corrie.

Winnipeg entered the interprovincial playdowns after they eliminated the two-time Dominion champions Norwood Wanderers FC in the Manitoba Final. Winnipeg then beat Fort William CPR in the Semifinals and Toronto Lancashire in the Dominion Final. Toronto reached the Final after they beat Montréal Grand Trunk FC.

Only four regions took part in the 1915 Connaught Cup Series: Manitoba and New Ontario in the West; Ontario and Québec in the East. It was the last Connaught Cup Series until the end of the Great War.

CHAMPIONS : WINNIPEG SCOTTISH FC

1915 Winnipeg Scottish FC : GK Alex Ross; Alec Dic, George Gardiner; Howard Wood, Bill Innes, Andy Campbell; Jocko Anderson, William Corrie, George Mair, John Plenderleith, Charles Forsyth. Manager Dan McNeil. Injured captain Billy Anderson.

MANITOBA SECTION	PROVINCIAL WINNERS	SCORE	RUNNERS UP
1915-07-24 Winnipeg, MB	Winnipeg Scottish FC D	1-1 D	Norwood Wanderers FC
1915-07-26 Winnipeg, MB	Winnipeg Scottish FC D	0-0 D	Norwood Wanderers FC
1915-07-27 Winnipeg, MB	Winnipeg Scottish FC W	2-0 L	Norwood Wanderers FC
CONNAUGHT CUP SERIES	**HOME TEAM**	**SCORE**	**AWAY TEAM**
1915-08-06 Winnipeg, MB	Winnipeg Scottish FC W	1-0 L	Fort William CPR
1915-08-07 Winnipeg, MB	Winnipeg Scottish FC W	2-1 L	Fort William CPR
CONNAUGHT CUP FINAL	**CHAMPIONS**	**SCORE**	**RUNNERS UP**
1915-08-11 Toronto, ON	Toronto Lancashire FC D	0-0 D	Winnipeg Scottish FC
1915-08-12 Toronto, ON	Toronto Lancashire FC L	1-6 W	Winnipeg Scottish FC

Winnipeg Scottish FC won 6-1 on aggregate to capture the Connaught Cup Series.
Winnipeg goals scored by George Mair (two), Charles Forsyth (two), Billy Corrie and Jocko Anderson.
Hero of the Connaught Cup Series : inside left Johnny Plenderleith.

Montréal Grand Trunk FC 1919
FIRST DOMINION CHAMPIONSHIP

14-16 AUGUST - NATIONAL GROUNDS & WESTMOUNT PARK
Montréal won first Cup after Great War

After three years without a champion because of the Great War, Montréal Grand Trunk FC became the first Eastern team to capture the Connaught Cup as Dominion champions. Across two matches in three days, Montréal won 3-1 on aggregate with a pair of wins in their home city.

Across two weeks in August, the railway men eliminated Montréal Highlanders in the Québec Final, Toronto Old Country in the Eastern Final, and the Winnipeg Great War Veterans in the Dominion Final. Their last match drew 6,000 spectators to Westmount Park.

Just like it was four years earlier, only four regions participated in the Dominion of Canada Football Championship: Manitoba and New Ontario in the West; Ontario and Québec in the East. Winnipeg beat Port Arthur Pascoes in the West Final.

Two months after winning the Connaught Cup, Montréal Grand Trunk FC won the 1919 Québec Cup with a 2-1 victory over Montréal CPR in the provincial championship.

CHAMPIONS : MONTRÉAL GRAND TRUNK FC
1919 Montréal Grand Trunk FC : GK Bobby Harris; Jimmy McLagan, W. Frier; Alec Rae, Chic Craigie, J. Jones; Artie Woutersz, Jimmy McLeish, Bill Worsley, Eddie Stott, Alec Smith. Missed Final. Davie Adamson (Injured), D. Adams, W. Adams, G. McCann, Johnny Rooney.

QUÉBEC SECTION	PROVINCIAL WINNERS	SCORE	RUNNERS UP
1919-08-02 Montréal, QC	Montréal Grand Trunk FC	W 4-1 L	Montréal Highlanders
CONNAUGHT CUP SERIES	**HOME TEAM**	**SCORE**	**AWAY TEAM**
1919-08-06 Toronto, ON	Toronto Old Country	W 4-1 L	Montréal Grand Trunk FC
1919-08-09 Montréal, QC	Montréal Grand Trunk FC	W 5-0 L	Toronto Old Country
CONNAUGHT CUP FINAL	**CHAMPIONS**	**SCORE**	**RUNNERS UP**
1919-08-14 Montréal, QC	Montréal Grand Trunk FC	W 2-1 L	Winnipeg Great War Vets
1919-08-16 Montréal, QC	Montréal Grand Trunk FC	W 1-0 L	Winnipeg Great War Vets

Montréal Grand Trunk FC won 3-1 on aggregate to capture the Connaught Cup Series.
Montréal goals in the Final: Winnipeg own goal, Jimmy McLeish; Eddie Stott.
Hero of the Connaught Cup Series : outside left Alec Smith.

CANADIAN SOCCER HISTORY
MEN'S AMATEUR FOOTBALL CHAMPIONS

1920s

– CONNAUGHT CUP

1920 *Hamilton Westinghouse*
FIRST DOMINION CHAMPIONSHIP

4-6 SEPTEMBER 1920 - HARVESTER PARK & VARSITY STADIUM

Gilvear scored Cup winner in extra time

Hamilton Westinghouse FC came from behind to capture the 1920 Connaught Cup with a 2-1 victory in extra time over Winnipeg Brittania. Billy Gilvear scored both goals in the last match of the series, the 1-1 equaliser in the 55th minute and the 2-1 winner in the 95th minute. Winnipeg were reduced to nine men in extra time because of injuries.

After Hamilton eliminated Toronto Willys Overland in the Ontario Cup, they beat Montréal CPR in the Eastern Final. The proposed three-team Final between Hamilton, Fort William and Winnipeg in August failed to determine a champion, so Hamilton advanced to the new Final and Winnipeg beat Fort William in an elimination series. Hamilton then beat Winnipeg Brittania in the September Final.

Hamilton captain Albert "Tiny" Thombs was the hero of the 1920 Final and he was the top scorer of the interprovincial playdowns with four goals in six matches across three rounds.

CHAMPIONS : HAMILTON WESTINGHOUSE FC

1920 Hamilton Westinghouse FC : GK A. Coombe; A. McEwan, Tommy Craig; Johnny Ure, D. Burns, Tommy Gardiner; Billy Gilvear, W. Jones, Peter Pascoe, T. Pilkington, Tiny Thombs captain. Missed Final : Billy Adair, T. Garside, E. Jones, W. Sinclair.

ONTARIO CUP FINAL	HOME TEAM	SCORE	AWAY TEAM
1920-07-03 Toronto, ON	Toronto Willys-Overland	L 2-3 W	Hamilton Westinghouse
CONNAUGHT CUP SERIES	**TEAM**	**SCORE**	**TEAM**
1920-07-27 Montréal, QC	Hamilton Westinghouse FC	L 1-2 W	Montréal CPR
1920-07-30 Toronto, ON	Hamilton Westinghouse FC	W 3-1 L	Montréal CPR

Hamilton Westinghouse FC won 4-3 on aggregate to eliminate Montréal CPR

1920-08-02 Toronto, ON	Hamilton Westinghouse FC	L 1-2 W	Fort William CPR
1920-08-05 Toronto, ON	Hamilton Westinghouse FC	W 2-0 L	Winnipeg Brittania

Hamilton advanced to the Final from a three-team series with Fort William and Winnipeg.

CONNAUGHT CUP FINAL	CHAMPIONS	SCORE	RUNNERS UP
1920-09-04 Hamilton, ON	Hamilton Westinghouse FC	D 0-0 D	Winnipeg Brittania
1920-09-06 Toronto, ON	Hamilton Westinghouse FC	W 2-1 L	Winnipeg Brittania

Hamilton Westinghouse FC won 2-1 on aggregate to capture the Connaught Cup Series.
Both Hamilton goals scored in the Final by Billy Gilvear.
Hero of the Connaught Cup Series : outside left Albert "Tiny" Thombs.

Toronto Scottish FC
FIRST DOMINION CHAMPIONSHIP 1921

3-6 AUGUST 1921 - BROADVIEW FIELD & ISLAND STADIUM IN TORONTO

MacDonald scored winner in Toronto

Toronto Scottish FC won the first coast-to-coast Dominion of Canada Football Championship after they beat British Columbia challengers Ladysmith FC in the 1921 Final. Toronto scored all four goals in the Final while goalkeeper Smith posted back-to-back clean sheets.

For the first time, eight regions from across Canada were represented in the first round of the Dominion of Canada Football Championship: Ladysmith beat Alberta's Calgary Callies; Saskatchewan's Regina Post beat Manitoba's Fort Rouge Rangers; Ontario's Toronto Scottish FC beat New Ontario's Fort William; and Québec's Montréal CPR beat Nova Scotia's Halifax Shipyards. Ladysmith then eliminated Regina while Toronto eliminated Montréal in the Semifinals.

Toronto captain Geordie Campbell was the hero of the Final while Hector MacDonald was the top scorer of the interprovincial playdowns with 10 goals in six matches (including two in the Final).

CHAMPIONS : TORONTO SCOTTISH FC
1921 Toronto Scottish FC : GK Smith; Geordie Campbell, George Houison; Harry Acourt captain, Alex McCall, Billy Sim; Harry Anderson, Bobby Bruce, Hector McDonald, Ernie Fidler, Aiken. Manager Dave Lumsden. Missed Final Match : Teddy Young (injured).

ONTARIO CUP FINAL	HOME TEAM	SCORE	AWAY TEAM
1921-07-02 Toronto, ON	Toronto Scottish FC	W 4-1	L Hamilton ILP
CONNAUGHT CUP SERIES	**TEAM**	**SCORE**	**TEAM**
1921-07-13 Fort William, ON	Fort William	L 0-4	W Toronto Scottish FC
1921-07-16 Toronto, ON	Toronto Scottish FC	W 11-0	L Fort William

Toronto Scottish FC won 15-0 on aggregate to eliminate Fort William in the Quarterfinals.

1921-07-23 Montréal, QC	Montréal CPR	D 2-2	D Toronto Scottish FC
1921-07-30 Toronto, ON	Toronto Scottish FC	W 5-0	L Montréal CPR

Toronto Scottish FC won 7-2 on aggregate to eliminate Montréal CPR in the Semifinals.

CONNAUGHT CUP FINAL	CHAMPIONS	SCORE	RUNNERS UP
1921-08-03 Toronto, ON	Toronto Scottish FC	W 3-0	L Ladysmith FC
1921-08-06 Toronto, ON	Toronto Scottish FC	W 1-0	L Ladysmith FC

Toronto Scottish FC won 4-0 on aggregate to capture the Connaught Cup Series.
Toronto goals: Hector MacDonald, Teddy Young, Ernie Fidler; Hector MacDonald.
Hero of the Connaught Cup Series : right back Geordie Campbell

— CONNAUGHT CUP

1922 Calgary Hillhurst FC
FIRST DOMINION CHAMPIONSHIP

10 TO 12 AUGUST 1922 - SCOTTISH FIELD IN TORONTO

Hillhurst won Dominion title for Calgary

Hillhurst FC brought the Connaught Cup home to Calgary after they beat Toronto Ulster United FC in the 1922 Dominion of Canada Football Championship. Hillhurst FC won the series 2-1 on aggregate with both matches played at Scottish Field in Toronto. Ulster played most of the second leg with just nine men after two of their players suffered injuries.

Calgary goalkeeper Andy Wilson was the hero of the 1922 Final and he posted a 0-0 clean sheet in the last match. Fred Deluce and Sammy Gough scored the Calgary goals in the opener. Across the three rounds in the interprovincial playdowns, Bernie Cartwright led all players with five goals in seven matches.

Eight weeks after they captured the Connaught Cup, Calgary Hillhurst FC beat Edmonton South Side in the Alberta Cup Final for the Bennett Shield.

CHAMPIONS : CALGARY HILLHURST FC
1922 Calgary Hillhurst FC : GK Andy Wilson; Freddie Foster, Bobby Stephen; Roy Austin, Andy Mitchell, Geordie Scott; Fred Deluce, Sammy Gough, Stan Wakelyn, Bernie Cartwright, Johnny Wright. Manager Bob Gallagher. Missed Final: Harry Banks, George Davis, Ed Wakelyn.

ALBERTA SECTION	HOME TEAM	SCORE	AWAY TEAM
1922-07-08 Edmonton, AB	Edmonton Great War Veterans L	1-3 W	Calgary Hillhurst FC
CONNAUGHT CUP SERIES	**HOME TEAM**	**SCORE**	**AWAY TEAM**
1922-07-14 Calgary, AB	Calgary Hillhurst FC L	1-2 W	Nanaimo City FC
1922-07-15 Calgary, AB	Calgary Hillhurst FC W	3-1 L	Nanaimo City FC
Calgary Hillhurst FC won 4-3 on aggregate to eliminate Nanaimo City FC in the Quarterfinals.			
1922-08-04 Winnipeg, MB	United Weston FC D	1-1 D	Calgary Hillhurst FC
1922-08-05 Winnipeg, MB	United Weston FC D	1-1 D	Calgary Hillhurst FC
1922-08-07 Winnipeg, MB	United Weston FC L	1-2 W	Calgary Hillhurst FC
Calgary Hillhurst FC won 4-3 on aggregate to eliminate United Weston FC in the Semifinals.			
CONNAUGHT CUP FINAL	**CHAMPIONS**	**SCORE**	**RUNNERS UP**
1922-08-10 Toronto, ON	Toronto Ulster United FC L	1-2 W	Calgary Hillhurst FC
1922-08-12 Toronto, ON	Toronto Ulster United FC D	0-0 D	Calgary Hillhurst FC

Calgary Hillhurst FC won 2-1 on aggregate to capture the Connaught Cup Series.
Calgary goals in the first leg scored by Fred Deluce and Sammy Gough.
Hero of the Connaught Cup Series : goalkeeper Andy Wilson.

Nanaimo City FC 1923
FIRST DOMINION CHAMPIONSHIP

4 TO 8 AUGUST 1923 - CARRUTHERS PARK IN WINNIPEG
Fowler scored Nanaimo's series winner

Nanaimo City FC won the Connaught Cup after they beat Montréal CPR by a single goal in the 1923 Dominion of Canada Football Championship. The Vancouver Island-based club won the series 2-1 on aggregate after Alex Fowler scored the match winner in the third and final match.

Dickie Stobbart was the hero of the 1923 Final and he scored the 1-0 match winner from the penalty spot in the series opener. Goalkeeper Tommy Routledge had two clean sheets in the Final.

Three months before they captured the 1923 Connaught Cup, Nanaimo City FC beat the University of British Columbia for the Province Cup at the end of April. In the BC Final for the Dominion series, Nanaimo City beat Vancouver Island's Cumberland FC by a single goal.

CHAMPIONS : NANAIMO CITY FC
1923 Nanaimo City FC Wanderers : GK Tommy Routledge; George Linn, Billy Bell; Angus McMillan, James McDougall captain, Dickie Stobbart; Dave Minto, Tommy Dickenson, J. Hines, Edward Appleby, Alex Fowler. Manager Jimmy Watson. Missed last match: Bobby Husband, Romeo Zaccarelli.

BRITISH COLUMBIA SECTION	HOME TEAM	SCORE	AWAY TEAM
1923-07-07 Nanaimo, BC	Nanaimo City FC	W 1-0	L Cumberland
CONNAUGHT CUP SERIES	**TEAM**	**SCORE**	**TEAM**
1923-07-20 Calgary, AB	Coleman	L 1-2	W Nanaimo City FC
1923-07-21 Calgary, AB	Coleman	L 1-3	W Nanaimo City FC
Nanaimo City FC won 5-2 on aggregate to eliminate Coleman in the Quarterfinals.			
1923-07-26 Winnipeg, MB	Fort Rouge Rangers	L 1-2	W Nanaimo City FC
1923-07-28 Winnipeg, MB	Fort Rouge Rangers	D 0-0	D Nanaimo City FC
Nanaimo City FC won 2-1 on aggregate to eliminate Fort Rouge in the Semifinals.			
CONNAUGHT CUP FINAL	**CHAMPIONS**	**SCORE**	**RUNNERS UP**
1923-08-04 Winnipeg, MB	Nanaimo City FC	W 1-0	L Montréal CPR
1923-08-06 Winnipeg, MB	Nanaimo City FC	L 0-1	W Montréal CPR
1923-08-08 Winnipeg, MB	Nanaimo City FC	W 1-0	L Montréal CPR

Nanaimo City FC won 2-1 on aggregate to capture the Connaught Cup Series.
Nanaimo City FC goals by Dickie Stobbart (first match) and Alex Fowler (third match).
Hero of the Connaught Cup Series : left half Dickie Stobbart.

1924 United Weston FC
FIRST DOMINION CHAMPIONSHIP

24 TO 26 JULY 1924 - CARRUTHERS PARK IN WINNIPEG

United Weston beat Beloeil for first Cup

United Weston FC won the 1924 Connaught Cup after they beat Beloeil Canadian Explosives in the Dominion of Canada Football Championship. The Winnipeg-based club won the series 3-2 on aggregate after both a 3-2 win and a 0-0 draw.

Centre half Bill Matthews was the hero of the 1924 Final and he earned Player of the Match honours in the 0-0 draw when goalkeeper Eddie Derby posted the clean sheet. Weston's Alex Slidders and Beloeil's Jack Renfrew co-led the tournament with five goals each.

Before United Weston FC entered the interprovincial playdowns for the Connaught Cup, they lost the 1924 Manitoba Cup in early June on a single goal to Winnipeg CPR. They turned around to beat Winnipeg Celtic FC in the Manitoba Final for the Connaught Cup Series.

CHAMPIONS : UNITED WESTON FC

1924 United Weston FC : GK Eddie Derby; Art King captain, Dan King; Johnny Fox, Bill Matthews, Jock McNeil; Scotty Lang, Jimmy Derby, Alex Slidders, Dougie Clark, Gregor Grant. Missed Final : J. McKenzie.

MANITOBA SECTION	PROVINCIAL WINNERS	SCORE	RUNNERS UP
1924-06-28 Winnipeg, MB	United Weston FC D	2-2 D	Winnipeg Celtic FC
1924-06-30 Winnipeg, MB	United Weston FC W	1-0 L	Winnipeg Celtic FC
CONNAUGHT CUP SERIES	**HOME TEAM**	**SCORE**	**AWAY TEAM**
1924-07-04 Winnipeg, MB	United Weston FC W	1-0 L	Moose Jaw CPR
1924-07-05 Winnipeg, MB	United Weston FC W	2-1 L	Moose Jaw CPR
United Weston FC won 3-1 on aggregate to eliminate Moose Jaw CPR in the Quarterfinals.			
1924-07-19 Winnipeg, MB	United Weston FC D	0-0 D	Cumberland FC
1924-07-22 Winnipeg, MB	United Weston FC W	2-0 L	Cumberland FC
United Weston FC won 2-0 on aggregate to eliminate Cumberland FC in the Semifinals.			
CONNAUGHT CUP FINAL	**CHAMPIONS**	**SCORE**	**RUNNERS UP**
1924-07-24 Winnipeg, MB	United Weston FC W	3-2 L	Canadian Explosives
1924-07-26 Winnipeg, MB	United Weston FC D	0-0 D	Canadian Explosives

United Weston FC won 3-2 on aggregate to capture the Connaught Cup Series.
United Weston FC goals scored in the first leg by Scotty Lang and Alex Slidders (two).
Hero of the Connaught Cup Series : centre half Bill Matthews.

Toronto Ulster United FC
FIRST DOMINION CHAMPIONSHIP

25 TO 29 JULY 1925 - CARRUTHERS PARK IN WINNIPEG

Ulster won Cup after brace by Lavery

Toronto Ulster United FC won the Connaught Cup after they beat former champions Nanaimo City FC in the 1925 Dominion of Canada Football Championship. Ulster won the series 3-1 on aggregate with all three Toronto goals scored by Bobby Lavery.

Jimmy Moir was the hero of the 1925 Final. He earned Player of the Match honours in the second match and got an assist on Lavery's last goal in the third match.

Across the three rounds of interprovincial playdowns, goalkeeper Smith posted four clean sheets, including two in the Final. He also posted a decisive clean sheet against Montréal Carsteel FC in the opening round.

Two months after winning their Dominion title, Ulster finished as runners up in the Interprovincial League playoffs by a single goal to Carsteel FC.

CHAMPIONS : TORONTO ULSTER UNITED FC
1925 Toronto Ulster United FC : GK Smith; Fred Williams, Walter Rankin; Billy Bissett, Joe Clulow, Angus Watt; Tommy Johnson, Phil Lavery, Bob Lavery captain, Sammy Grant, Jimmy Moir. Manager R. Torrans. Missed last match: Gervan. Missed Final: Art Barron, Bill Wollacott.

ONTARIO SECTION	PROVINCIAL WINNERS	SCORE	RUNNERS UP
1925-07-04 Toronto, ON	Toronto Ulster United FC	W 5-0	L Toronto Scottish FC
CONNAUGHT CUP SERIES	**HOME TEAM**	**SCORE**	**TEAM**
1925-07-11 Montréal, QC	Montréal Carsteel FC	W 1-0	L Toronto Ulster United FC
1925-07-18 Toronto, ON	Toronto Ulster United FC	W 2-0	L Montréal Carsteel FC
Toronto Ulster United FC won 3-0 on aggregate to eliminate Montréal in the Quarterfinals.			
1925-07-23 Fort William, ON	Fort William War Veterans	L 0-1	W Toronto Ulster United FC
Toronto Ulster United FC won 1-0 to eliminate Fort William in the Semifinals.			
CONNAUGHT CUP FINAL	**CHAMPIONS**	**SCORE**	**RUNNERS UP**
1925-07-25 Winnipeg, MB	Toronto Ulster United FC	D 0-0	D Nanaimo City FC
1925-07-27 Winnipeg, MB	Toronto Ulster United FC	D 1-1	D Nanaimo City FC
1925-07-29 Winnipeg, MB	Toronto Ulster United FC	W 2-0	L Nanaimo City FC

Toronto Ulster United FC won 3-1 on aggregate to capture the Connaught Cup Series.
All three Toronto Ulster United FC goals in the Final scored by Bobby Lavery.
Hero of the Connaught Cup Series : outside left Jimmy Moir.

- CHALLENGE TROPHY

1926 *United Weston FC*
SECOND DOMINION CHAMPIONSHIP

29 JULY TO 4 AUGUST 1926 - CARRUTHERS PARK IN WINNIPEG

Weston won the new Challenge Trophy

United Weston FC won their second title in three years after they beat Cumberland FC in the 1926 Dominion of Canada Football Championship. United Weston FC won the series 3-2 on aggregate after Johnny Lang scored the series winner in the last match.

Goalkeeper Eddie Derby was the hero of the 1926 Final after he posted two clean sheets in four matches against Cumberland FC. Across three rounds in the interprovincial playdowns, Duncan Watson led all players with nine goals in eight matches.

United Weston FC reached the playdowns after they beat Irish FC in the Manitoba Final for the Connaught Cup Series. It was Weston's fourth qualification to the series in five years.

CHAMPIONS : UNITED WESTON FC

1926 United Weston FC : GK Eddie Derby; Dan King captain, Art King captain; Art Slidders, Bob McIntosh, Jock McNeil; Scotty Lang, George Hutchinson, Duncan Watson, Johnny Lang, Dusty Miller. Missed last match: Borland. Missed Final: Bill Matthews (injured), Patrick O'Kane.

MANITOBA SECTION	PROVINCIAL WINNERS	SCORE	RUNNERS UP
1926-06-26 Winnipeg, MB	United Weston FC	struck	Winnipeg Irish FC
1926-07-10 Winnipeg, MB	United Weston FC W	4-0 L	Winnipeg Irish FC
CONNAUGHT CUP SERIES	**HOME TEAM**	**SCORE**	**AWAY TEAM**
1926-07-17 Winnipeg, MB	United Weston FC W	4-1 L	Fort William Veterans
1926-07-19 Winnipeg, MB	United Weston FC W	5-0 L	Fort William Veterans
United Weston FC won 9-1 on aggregate to eliminate Fort William in the Quarterfinals.			
1926-07-24 Winnipeg, MB	United Weston FC W	3-1 L	Toronto Willys-Overland
1926-07-26 Winnipeg, MB	United Weston FC W	5-2 L	Toronto Willys-Overland
United Weston FC won 8-3 on aggregate to eliminate Toronto in the Semifinals.			
CHALLENGE TROPHY FINAL	**CHAMPIONS**	**SCORE**	**RUNNERS UP**
1926-07-29 Winnipeg, MB	United Weston FC D	0-0 D	Cumberland FC
1926-07-31 Winnipeg, MB	United Weston FC D	1-1 D	Cumberland FC
1926-08-02 Winnipeg, MB	United Weston FC D	1-1 D	Cumberland FC
1926-08-04 Winnipeg, MB	United Weston FC W	1-0 L	Cumberland FC

United Weston FC won 3-2 on aggregate to capture the Challenge Trophy.
United Weston FC goals scored by George Hutchinson, Jock McNeil, and Johnny Lang.
Hero of the Connaught Cup Series : goalkeeper Eddie Derby.

Nanaimo City FC
SECOND DOMINION CHAMPIONSHIP 1927

1 TO 3 AUGUST 1927 - CARRUTHERS PARK IN WINNIPEG

Nanaimo won second Challenge Trophy

Nanaimo City FC won their second title in five years after they beat Fort William Legion in the 1927 Dominion of Canada Football Championship. Nanaimo City FC won the series 14-1 on aggregate after back-to-back wins in Winnipeg.

Dave Cowie was the hero of the 1927 Final when he scored five goals in two matches (including a hat trick in the opener). Across six matches in the interprovincial playdowns, Cowie and John Sandland scored six goals each while Alex Fowler and Nelson Wilson scored five goals each.

Before the Connaught Cup Series, Nanaimo City FC were awarded the 1927 Province Cup after Powell River refused to feature in the provincial championship. Then in the BC Final for the Dominion series, Nanaimo City FC eliminated Westminster Royals FC to enter the interprovincial playdowns.

CHAMPIONS : NANAIMO CITY FC

1927 Nanaimo City FC Wanderers : GK Tommy Routledge; Len Perry, Alex Thompson; Jimmy Knight, Neil MacFarlane captain, Jock Clarke; Nelson Wilson, John Sandland, Dave Cowie, Joe Milburn, Alex Fowler. Manager Archie Hannah. Missed Final: Alexander, Dave Minto, Dickie Stobbart.

BRITISH COLUMBIA SECTION	PROVINCIAL WINNERS	SCORE	RUNNERS UP
1927-07-16 Vancouver, BC	Westminster Royals FC D	0-0 D	Nanaimo City FC
1927-07-18 Vancouver, BC	Westminster Royals FC	?	Nanaimo City FC
1927-07-20 Vancouver, BC	Westminster Royals FC L	1-4 W	Nanaimo City FC
CONNAUGHT CUP SERIES	**TEAM**	**SCORE**	**TEAM**
1927-07-23 Edmonton, AB	Edmonton Canadian Legion	0-2	Nanaimo City FC
1927-07-25 Edmonton, AB	Edmonton Canadian Legion	2-2	Nanaimo City FC

Nanaimo City FC won 4-2 on aggregate to eliminate Edmonton in the Quarterfinals.

1927-07-27 Winnipeg, MB	Saskatoon Sons of England	2-5	Nanaimo City FC
1927-07-29 Winnipeg, MB	Saskatoon Sons of England	1-8	Nanaimo City FC

Nanaimo City FC won 13-3 on aggregate to eliminate Saskatoon in the Semifinals.

CHALLENGE TROPHY FINAL	CHAMPIONS	SCORE	RUNNERS UP
1927-08-01 Winnipeg, MB	Nanaimo City FC	9-0	Fort William Legion
1927-08-03 Winnipeg, MB	Nanaimo City FC	5-1	Fort William Legion

Nanaimo City FC won 14-1 on aggregate to capture the Challenge Trophy.
Hero of the Connaught Cup Series : centre forward Dave Cowie.

■ CHALLENGE TROPHY

1928 Westminster Royals FC
FIRST DOMINION CHAMPIONSHIP

28 JULY TO 1 AUGUST 1928 - CARRUTHERS PARK IN WINNIPEG

Coulter scored four as Royals won title

Westminster Royals FC won their first Dominion of Canada Football Championship after they beat former champions Montréal CNR in the 1928 Final. They won the opener 3-2, then wrapped up the series in the third match with a 6-1 victory on the strength of Jock Coulter's four goals.

Coulter was the hero of the 1928 Final when he scored seven goals in three matches, including the first-ever hat trick scored in the last match of the Final. Coulter led all players with 15 goals in six interprovincial matches.

Before the Connaught Cup Series, New Westminster won the 1927-28 Mainland Cup with a 2-0 victory over Vancouver St. Saviours in May. In the provincial championship, they were eliminated by Woodfibre in the first round in March.

CHAMPIONS : WESTMINSTER ROYALS FC

1928 Westminster Royals FC : GK Stanley Ball; Alexander Strang, George Anderson; Les Rimmer, George Russell, Austin Delany; Adam Kerr, Dickie Stobbart, Jock Coulter, Dave Turner, Harry Chapman. Manager Don Earl McLeod. Missed last match: GK Andy Roots, GK Aubrey Sanford, Jimmy Smith, Tom Taylor, Tommy Trotter. Missed Final series: Robert McDougall.

BRITISH COLUMBIA SECTION	PROVINCIAL WINNERS	SCORE	RUNNERS UP
1928-07-07 Vancouver, BC	Westminster Royals FC	W 5-2 L	Vancouver St. Paul's FC
CONNAUGHT CUP SERIES	**HOME TEAM**	**SCORE**	**AWAY TEAM**
1928-07-14 Vancouver, BC	Westminster Royals FC	4-0	Edmonton Cdn. Legion
1928-07-16 Vancouver, BC	Westminster Royals FC	9-6	Edmonton Cdn. Legion

Westminster Royals FC won 13-6 on aggregate to eliminate Edmonton in the Quarterfinals.

1928-07-23 Winnipeg, MB	Winnipeg Westbrook	1-7	Westminster Royals FC
1928-07-25 Winnipeg, MB	Winnipeg Westbrook	0-2	Westminster Royals FC

Westminster Royals FC won 9-1 on aggregate to eliminate Winnipeg in the Semifinals.

CHALLENGE TROPHY FINAL	**CHAMPIONS**	**SCORE**	**RUNNERS UP**
1928-07-28 Winnipeg, MB	Westminster Royals FC	W 3-2 L	Montréal CNR
1928-07-30 Winnipeg, MB	Westminster Royals FC	L 1-2 W	Montréal CNR
1928-08-01 Winnipeg, MB	Westminster Royals FC	W 6-1 L	Montréal CNR

Westminster Royals FC won the best-of-three series to capture the Challenge Trophy.
Hero of the Connaught Cup Series : centre forward Jock Coulter.

Montréal Canadian National
SECOND DOMINION CHAMPIONSHIP 1929

29 TO 31 JULY 1929 - CARRUTHERS PARK IN WINNIPEG

CNR beat the hosts for Dominion title

Montréal Canadian National Railway won the Dominion of Canada Football Championship in 1929 after they posted back-to-back wins over the two-time champions United Weston FC. Montréal scored nine goals while goalkeeper Jimmy Nelson posted two clean sheets against the Winnipeg club at Carruthers Park.

Bill Finlayson was the hero of the 1929 Final when he scored four goals and two assists in two matches. Across three rounds, he led all players with seven goals in six interprovincial matches. Denmark international Poul Nielsen scored four goals in the playdowns while Joseph Williams scored three goals in the Final.

Canadian National Railway, previously known as Grand Trunk FC, won the National League's delayed 1928 Atholstan Cup in April 1929 and the 1929 Atholstan Cup in October 1929. Montréal were Dominion runners up to Westminster Royals FC in both 1928 and 1930.

CHAMPS : MONTRÉAL CANADIAN NATIONAL RAILWAY

1929 Montréal CNR : GK Jimmy Nelson; Harry Barnes, James Duguid; Frank Henderson, Peter Keir captain, Bob Campbell; Joseph Williams, Dave Meldrum, Bill Finlayson, Poul Nielsen, Jack Green. Manager : Harry Payne. Missed Final: J. Graham, Low, Murphy, J. Naismith, James Turnbull.

QUÉBEC SECTION	PROVINCIAL WINNERS	SCORE	RUNNERS UP
1929-07-01 Montréal, QC	Montréal CNR	W 5-0 L	Montréal CPR
CONNAUGHT CUP SERIES	**HOME TEAM**	**SCORE**	**AWAY TEAM**
1929-07-20 Montréal, QC	Montréal CNR	3-2	Oshawa General Motors
1929-07-22 Oshawa, ON	Oshawa General Motors	1-1	Montréal CNR
Montréal CNR won 4-3 on aggregate to eliminate Oshawa in the Quarterfinals.			
1929-07-25 Fort William, ON	Fort William Canadian Legion	2-5	Montréal CNR
1929-07-27 Fort William, ON	Fort William Canadian Legion	2-1	Montréal CNR
Montréal CNR won 6-4 on aggregate to eliminate Fort William in the Semifinals.			
CHALLENGE TROPHY FINAL	**HOME TEAM**	**SCORE**	**AWAY TEAM**
1929-07-29 Winnipeg, MB	United Weston FC	L 0-4 W	Montréal CNR
1929-07-31 Winnipeg, MB	United Weston FC	L 0-5 W	Montréal CNR

Montréal CNR won the best-of-three series to capture the Challenge Trophy.
Hero of the Connaught Cup Series : centre forward Bill Finlayson.

CANADIAN SOCCER HISTORY
MEN'S AMATEUR FOOTBALL CHAMPIONS

1930s

1930  Westminster Royals FC
SECOND DOMINION CHAMPIONSHIP

29 JULY TO 2 AUGUST 1930 - CARRUTHERS PARK IN WINNIPEG

Coulter scored New Westminster winner

Westminster Royals FC won their second Dominion of Canada Football Championship in three years after they beat defending champions Montréal CNR in the 1930 Final. Jock Coulter scored the 1-0 series winner in the decisive third match.

Goalkeeper Aubrey Sanford was the hero of the 1930 Final and he posted 1-0 clean sheets in both the first and last matches of the series. Coulter scored the match winner in both victories and he led all players with eight goals in six interprovincial matches.

Before the Connaught Cup Series, Westminster Royals FC won the 1930 Province Cup after a 3-2 victory over Vancouver St. Andrews FC. They lost the 1930 Mainland Cup three weeks later after a 2-1 defeat to St. Andrews FC on 17 May.

CHAMPIONS : WESTMINSTER ROYALS FC

1930 Westminster Royals FC : GK Aubrey Sanford; George Anderson, James Waugh; Les Rimmer, Harold Stoddart, Austin Delany; Robert McDougall, Tommy Trotter, Jock Coulter, Dave Turner, Jack d'Easum. Manager Don Earl McLeod. Missed last match: Bob Peroni, Tom Taylor, Jack Wood. Missed Final: Tassin, Wall.

BRITISH COLUMBIA SECTION	PROVINCIAL WINNERS	SCORE	RUNNERS UP
1930-06-28 Vancouver, BC	Westminster Royals FC	W 4-1 L	Vancouver St. Saviours
CONNAUGHT CUP SERIES	**HOME TEAM**	**SCORE**	**AWAY TEAM**
1930-07-14 Vancouver, BC	Westminster Royals FC	W 2-1 L	Calgary Hillhurst
1930-07-16 Vancouver, BC	Westminster Royals FC	W 8-1 L	Calgary Hillhurst
Westminster Royals FC won 10-2 on aggregate to eliminate Calgary in the Quarterfinals.			
1930-07-24 Winnipeg, MB	Winnipeg Hearts	W 1-0 L	Westminster Royals FC
1930-07-26 Winnipeg, MB	Winnipeg Hearts	L 0-3 W	Westminster Royals FC
Westminster Royals FC won 3-1 on aggregate to eliminate Winnipeg in the Semifinals.			
CHALLENGE TROPHY FINAL	**CHAMPIONS**	**SCORE**	**RUNNERS UP**
1930-07-29 Winnipeg, MB	Westminster Royals FC	W 1-0 L	Montréal CNR
1930-07-31 Winnipeg, MB	Westminster Royals FC	L 0-5 W	Montréal CNR
1930-08-02 Winnipeg, MB	Westminster Royals FC	W 1-0 L	Montréal CNR

Westminster Royals FC won the best-of-three series to capture the Challenge Trophy.
Both Westminster goals scored in the Final series by Jock Coulter.
Hero of the Connaught Cup Series : goalkeeper Aubrey Sanford.

CHALLENGE TROPHY

Westminster Royals FC  1931
THIRD DOMINION CHAMPIONSHIP

30 JULY TO 3 AUGUST 1931 - CARRUTHERS PARK IN WINNIPEG

Royals established dynasty with third win

Westminster Royals FC won their third Dominion of Canada Football Championship in four years when they posted back-to-back wins over Toronto Scottish FC in the 1931 Final. They won the first match 2-0 and the second match 3-0 with back-to-back clean sheets posted by goalkeeper Aubrey Sanford.

Captain Dave Turner was the hero of the 1931 Final and he earned Player of the Match honours in the last match. Ernie Hammond scored in both matches and he led all players with six goals in six interprovincial matches.

Before the Connaught Cup Series, Westminster Royals FC won the 1931 Province Cup after a 4-1 victory over Esquimalt from Vancouver Island. They won the BC Final in the Dominion series with a 4-2 win over two-time Dominion champions Nanaimo City FC.

CHAMPIONS : WESTMINSTER ROYALS FC
1931 Westminster Royals FC : GK Aubrey Sanford; Cud Makepeace, Bill Hogg; Tommy Trotter, Harold Stoddart, Dickie Stobbart; Adam Kerr, Bill Findler, Ernie Hammond, Dave Turner captain, Jack d'Easum. Manager Don Earl McLeod. Missed Final: G. Babcock, Alex Sneddon. Missed playdowns through suspension: George Anderson, Jock Coulter, Austin Delany, Dan Kulai, Les Rimmer.

BRITISH COLUMBIA SECTION	PROVINCIAL WINNERS	SCORE	RUNNERS UP
1931-07-04 Vancouver, BC	Westminster Royals FC	W 4-2 L	Nanaimo City FC
CONNAUGHT CUP SERIES	**HOME TEAM**	**SCORE**	**AWAY TEAM**
1931-07-22 Edmonton, AB	Edmonton CNR	L 0-1 W	Westminster Royals FC
1931-07-23 Edmonton, AB	Edmonton CNR	L 1-2 W	Westminster Royals FC
Westminster Royals FC won 3-1 on aggregate to eliminate Edmonton in the Quarterfinals.			
1931-07-25 Winnipeg, MB	Winnipeg Irish	L 2-5 W	Westminster Royals FC
1931-07-27 Winnipeg, MB	Winnipeg Irish	W 2-1 L	Westminster Royals FC
Westminster Royals FC won 6-4 on aggregate to eliminate Winnipeg in the Semifinals.			
CHALLENGE TROPHY FINAL	**CHAMPIONS**	**SCORE**	**RUNNERS UP**
1931-07-30 Winnipeg, MB	Westminster Royals FC	W 2-0 L	Toronto Scottish FC
1931-08-03 Winnipeg, MB	Westminster Royals FC	W 3-0 L	Toronto Scottish FC

Westminster Royals FC won the best-of-three series to capture the Challenge Trophy.
Hero of the Connaught Cup Series : inside left Dave Turner.

— CHALLENGE TROPHY —

1932  Toronto Scottish FC
SECOND DOMINION CHAMPIONSHIP

28 TO 30 JULY 1932 - ULSTER STADIUM IN TORONTO

Stevens led Scottish to title in Toronto

Toronto Scottish FC won their second Dominion of Canada Football Championship after they beat North Shore United FC in the 1932 Final after back-to-back wins at Ulster Stadium. They won the first match 3-0 and the second match 2-1. Jimmy Winning scored the 2-1 match winner in the second match.

Andy Stevens was the hero of the 1932 Final when he scored three of Toronto's five goals. Across three rounds, Stevens led all players with seven goals in six interprovincial matches. Goalkeeper Hugh Wallace posted three clean sheets in the playdowns while centre half Billy Somers was a defensive stalwart in the Final against North Shore United FC.

Before the 1932 Connaught Cup Series, Toronto Scottish FC won the delayed 1931 Ontario Cup in June 1932. Stevens scored seven goals in the two-match series.

CHAMPIONS : TORONTO SCOTTISH FC
1932 Toronto Scottish FC : GK Hugh Wallace; Billy Conner, Jimmy Noke; Davie Weir, Billy Somers, Johnny Rogers; Bill McManus, Jimmy Winning, Andy Stevens, Norman Donald, Jimmy McIntyre. Missed last match: Johnny Cairns. Missed Final: George Erasmusson, Hector MacDonald.

ONTARIO SECTION	TEAM	SCORE	TEAM
1932-06-30 Toronto, ON	Toronto Scottish FC	2-0	Toronto TTC
1932-07-05 Toronto, ON	Toronto TTC	0-2	Toronto Scottish FC
CONNAUGHT CUP SERIES	**HOME TEAM**	**SCORE**	**AWAY TEAM**
1932-07-16 Toronto, ON	Toronto Scottish FC	3-0	Fort William Cdn. Legion
1932-07-18 Toronto, ON	Toronto Scottish FC	3-0	Fort William Cdn. Legion
Toronto Scottish FC won 6-0 on aggregate to eliminate Fort William in the Quarterfinals.			
1932-07-21 Toronto, ON	Toronto Scottish FC	5-1	Montréal Blue Bonnets
1932-07-23 Toronto, ON	Toronto Scottish FC	2-3	Montréal Blue Bonnets
Toronto Scottish FC won 7-4 on aggregate to eliminate Montréal in the Semifinals.			
CHALLENGE TROPHY FINAL	**HOME TEAM**	**SCORE**	**AWAY TEAM**
1932-07-28 Toronto, ON	Toronto Scottish FC W	3-0 L	North Shore United FC
1932-07-30 Toronto, ON	Toronto Scottish FC W	2-1 L	North Shore United FC

Toronto Scottish FC won the best-of-three series to capture the Challenge Trophy.
Hero of the Connaught Cup Series : centre forward Andy Stevens.

Toronto Scottish FC  1933
THIRD DOMINION CHAMPIONSHIP

3 TO 7 AUGUST 1933 - CARRUTHERS PARK IN WINNIPEG

Scottish repeated as Dominion champs

Toronto Scottish FC were back-to-back Dominion of Canada Football Championship winners after they beat the Prince Albert City Reds in the 1933 Final. All even after two draws, Toronto clinched the best-of-three series after they won the last match 3-0 at Winnipeg's Carruthers Park.

Hector MacDonald was the hero of the 1933 Final when he scored three of Toronto's five goals. Bill McManus, who scored the last goal of the Final, led all players with 10 goals in nine interprovincial matches. Stars Billy Somers and Andy Stevens, who scored in the earlier rounds, both missed the Final (Somers through injury and work reasons, Stevens on an account of bereavement after the passing of his mother).

CHAMPIONS : TORONTO SCOTTISH FC
1933 Toronto Scottish FC : GK Hugh Wallace; Davie Weir, Jimmy Noke; Johnny Graham, Harry Phillips, Robert Manson; Angus MacDonald, Hector MacDonald, Jack Patterson, Norman Donald, Bill McManus. Missed Final: Billy Grassam, captain Billy Somers (injured), Andy Stevens (absent, bereavement).

ONTARIO SECTION		HOME TEAM	SCORE		AWAY TEAM
1933-07-01	Brantford, ON	Brantford City	D 2-2	D	Toronto Scottish FC
1933-07-05	Toronto, ON	Toronto Scottish FC	W 3-1	L	Brantford City
1933-07-08	Toronto, ON	Toronto Scottish FC	W 8-1	L	Brantford City
CONNAUGHT CUP SERIES		**HOME TEAM**	**SCORE**		**AWAY TEAM**
1933-07-20	Toronto, ON	Toronto Scottish FC	0-0		McIntyre Mines
1933-07-22	Toronto, ON	Toronto Scottish FC	3-3		McIntyre Mines
1933-07-24	Toronto, ON	Toronto Scottish FC	5-2		McIntyre Mines
Toronto Scottish FC won 8-5 on aggregate to eliminate McIntyre in the Quarterfinals.					
1933-07-27	Toronto, ON	Toronto Scottish FC	2-2		Montréal CNR
1933-07-29	Toronto, ON	Toronto Scottish FC	1-1		Montréal CNR
1933-07-31	Toronto, ON	Toronto Scottish FC	4-1		Montréal CNR
Toronto Scottish FC won 7-4 on aggregate to eliminate Montréal in the Semifinals.					
CHALLENGE TROPHY FINAL		**CHAMPIONS**	**SCORE**		**RUNNERS UP**
1933-08-03	Winnipeg, MB	Toronto Scottish FC	D 2-2	D	Prince Albert City Reds
1933-08-05	Winnipeg, MB	Toronto Scottish FC	D 0-0	D	Prince Albert City Reds
1933-08-07	Winnipeg, MB	Toronto Scottish FC	W 3-0	L	Prince Albert City Reds

Toronto Scottish FC won the best-of-three series to capture the Challenge Trophy.
Hero of the Connaught Cup Series : inside right Hector MacDonald.

■ CHALLENGE TROPHY

1934 *Verdun Park FC*
FIRST DOMINION CHAMPIONSHIP

11 TO 16 AUGUST 1934 - CARRUTHERS PARK IN WINNIPEG

Dempsey led Verdun to Dominion title

Verdun Park FC won the Dominion of Canada Football Championship after they beat the Prince Albert City Reds in the 1934 Final. Verdun won the first and third matches to clinch the best-of-three series.

Roland "Dempsey" Castonguay was the hero of the 1934 Final and he had both a goal and an assist in the two wins against Prince Albert. He finished the Connaught Cup Series with four goals in eight interprovincial matches while teammate Larry Fitzpatrick was the tournament leader with eight goals in eight matches (including three goals against Prince Albert). The Castonguay-Fitzpatrick duo either scored or assisted seven of Verdun's eight goals in the Final.

Before the Final, Verdun Park FC needed five matches to get past Northern Ontario side Frood Mines in the Eastern Final. The two sides drew four-straight matches before Verdun won the last match 3-1 on a series winner scored by Fitzpatrick (assisted by Castonguay).

CHAMPIONS : VERDUN PARK FC

1934 Verdun Park FC : GK Everett MacLean; Humphrey Payne captain, J. Lone; Jim MacKenzie, Billy Holmshaw, John Menary; Charlie Fitzpatrick, Billy Bennett, Larry Fitzpatrick, Tony Quinn, Roland Castonguay. Missed Final: James Duguid (injured), Allan Fitzpatrick, Davy Fitzpatrick.

QUÉBEC SECTION	PROVINCIAL WINNERS	SCORE	RUNNERS UP
1934-06-23 Montréal, QC	Verdun Park FC	W 2-0 L	Montréal Carsteel FC
CONNAUGHT CUP SERIES	**TEAM**	**SCORE**	**TEAM**
1934-07-21 Toronto, ON	Sudbury Frood Mines	D 2-2 D	Verdun Park FC
1934-07-23 Toronto, ON	Sudbury Frood Mines	D 1-1 D	Verdun Park FC
1934-07-25 Toronto, ON	Sudbury Frood Mines	D 2-2 D	Verdun Park FC
1934-07-28 Toronto, ON	Sudbury Frood Mines	D 0-0 D	Verdun Park FC
1934-07-30 Toronto, ON	Sudbury Frood Mines	L 1-3 W	Verdun Park FC
CHALLENGE TROPHY FINAL	**RUNNERS UP**	**SCORE**	**CHAMPIONS**
1934-08-11 Winnipeg, MB	Prince Albert City Reds	L 0-4 W	Verdun Park FC
1934-08-14 Winnipeg, MB	Prince Albert City Reds	W 2-0 L	Verdun Park FC
1934-08-16 Winnipeg, MB	Prince Albert City Reds	L 1-4 W	Verdun Park FC

Verdun Park FC won the best-of-three series to capture the Challenge Trophy.
Hero of the Connaught Cup Series : outside left Roland "Dempsey" Castonguay.

Montréal Aldred FC 1935
FIRST DOMINION CHAMPIONSHIP

19 TO 24 AUGUST 1935 - CARRUTHERS PARK IN WINNIPEG

Campbell scored Aldred's series winner

Montréal Aldred FC won the Dominion of Canada Football Championship after they beat two-time winners Nanaimo City FC in the 1935 Final. Tied through three matches, Montréal won the extended series after Bob Campbell scored the 1-0 series winner in the fourth and final match.

Charlie Fitzpatrick was the hero of the 1935 Final while his brother Larry led all scorers with eight goals in 11 interprovincial matches.

Just two weeks after winning the Dominion title, Aldred FC captured the Québec Cup with a 1-0 victory over Montréal Royal Victoria Hospital FC.

CHAMPIONS : MONTRÉAL ALDRED FC
1935 Montréal Aldred FC : GK Jimmy Nelson; Ronald Low, George White; Allan Fitzpatrick, Bert Lumsden, Bob Campbell captain; Charlie Fitzpatrick, Albert Bejshak, Larry Fitzpatrick, Paddy Fallon, Davey McLean. Substitutions: Joe Bardell, Tom McIntosh, Peter Keir. Missed Final: GK A. Bates, Bill Allison, Roland Castonguay, Charles Cook, Jas Craig, Andy Keir.

QUÉBEC SECTION		TEAM	SCORE	TEAM
1935-07-06	Montréal, QC	Montréal Aldred FC	3-0	Montréal Shell Oil FC
1935-07-09	Montréal, QC	Montréal Shell Oil FC	0-0	Montréal Aldred FC
CONNAUGHT CUP SERIES		**HOME TEAM**	**SCORE**	**AWAY TEAM**
1935-08-02	Montréal, QC	Montréal Aldred FC	6-0	Halifax St. George's
1935-08-03	Montréal, QC	Montréal Aldred FC	7-1	Halifax St. George's
Montréal Aldred FC won 13-1 on aggregate to eliminate Halifax in the first round.				
1935-08-07	Montréal, QC	Montréal Aldred FC	0-1	Sudbury Falconbridge
1935-08-09	Montréal, QC	Montréal Aldred FC	1-0	Sudbury Falconbridge
1935-08-10	Montréal, QC	Montréal Aldred FC	4-1	Sudbury Falconbridge
Montréal Aldred FC won 5-2 on aggregate to eliminate Sudbury in the second round.				
1935-08-13	Fort William, ON	Fort William Wanderers	0-2	Montréal Aldred FC
1935-08-15	Fort William, ON	Fort William Wanderers	1-2	Montréal Aldred FC
Montréal Aldred FC won 4-1 on aggregate to eliminate Fort William in the Semifinals.				
CHALLENGE TROPHY FINAL		**CHAMPIONS**	**SCORE**	**RUNNERS UP**
1935-08-19	Winnipeg, MB	Montréal Aldred FC W	3-2	L Nanaimo City FC
1935-08-21	Winnipeg, MB	Montréal Aldred FC L	3-7	W Nanaimo City FC
1935-08-23	Winnipeg, MB	Montréal Aldred FC D	1-1	D Nanaimo City FC
1935-08-24	Winnipeg, MB	Montréal Aldred FC W	1-0	L Nanaimo City FC

Montréal Aldred FC won the best-of-three series (four matches) to capture the Challenge Trophy. Hero of the Connaught Cup Series : outside right Charlie Fitzpatrick.

■ CHALLENGE TROPHY

1936  *Westminster Royals FC*
FOURTH DOMINION CHAMPIONSHIP

8 TO 12 AUGUST 1936 - CON JONES PARK IN VANCOUVER

Westminster won fourth Dominion title

Westminster Royals FC won their fourth Dominion of Canada Football Championship in nine years after they beat two-time winners United Weston FC in a best-of-three series. The Royals won the deciding match 3-0 on goals by Dave Turner, Johnny McKay and Jock Coulter while goalkeeper Stan Stronge posted the clean sheet at Con Jones Park in Vancouver.

Captain Turner was the hero of the 1936 Final with three goals and three assists in the three matches against United Weston FC. Coulter was the tournament's top scorer with 13 goals in four interprovincial matches, including seven goals in the 12-0 victory over Calgary Callies in the Western Final.

Before the Connaught Cup Series, Westminster Royals FC captured the 1936 Province Cup with a 4-2 victory over Nanaimo City FC. Coulter scored a hat trick. Westminster then beat North Shore United FC in the British Columbia Final to qualify for the interprovincial playdowns. Coulter scored two goals in the win.

CHAMPIONS : WESTMINSTER ROYALS FC

1936 Westminster Royals FC : GK Stan Stronge; George Anderson, Tommy McKibbin; Dot McPherson, Trevor Harvey, Jimmy Gemmell; Bill Findlay, Johnny McKay, Jock Coulter, Dave Turner captain, Ray Watchorn. Manager Les Rimmer. Missed last match: W. Gray, Walt Wheeler.

BRITISH COLUMBIA SECTION	PROVINCIAL WINNERS	SCORE	RUNNERS UP
1936-07-11 Vancouver, BC	Westminster Royals FC	W 3-1 L	North Shore United FC
CONNAUGHT CUP SERIES	**HOME TEAM**	**SCORE**	**AWAY TEAM**
1936-07-23 Vancouver, BC	Westminster Royals FC	2-1	Calgary Callies FC
1936-07-25 Vancouver, BC	Westminster Royals FC	12-0	Calgary Callies FC

Westminster Royals FC won 14-1 on aggregate to eliminate Calgary in the Semifinals.

CHALLENGE TROPHY FINAL	HOME TEAM	SCORE	AWAY TEAM
1936-08-08 Vancouver, BC	Westminster Royals FC	W 6-1 L	United Weston FC
1936-08-10 Vancouver, BC	Westminster Royals FC	L 1-2 W	United Weston FC
1936-08-12 Vancouver, BC	Westminster Royals FC	W 3-0 L	United Weston FC

Westminster Royals FC won the best-of-three series to capture the Challenge Trophy.
Hero of the Connaught Cup Series : inside left Dave Turner.

Vancouver Johnstons 1937
FIRST DOMINION CHAMPIONSHIP

29 JULY TO 2 AUGUST 1937 - CARRUTHERS PARK IN WINNIPEG

Johnston Nationals won Dominion title

Vancouver Johnston National Storage FC won the Dominion of Canada Football Championship after they beat former champions Toronto Ulster United FC in the 1937 Final. After Toronto won the first match, Vancouver posted back-to-back wins to capture the Challenge Trophy.

Swede Larson was the hero of the 1937 Final after he scored both the equaliser and 3-2 match winner in the deciding match of the series with Toronto. Larson was also Vancouver's leading scorer with six goals in eight interprovincial matches.

Two months before the Connaught Cup Series, Vancouver Johnston National Storage FC captured the 1937 Mainland Cup after a 4-0 victory over Kerrisdale. After the Connaught Cup Series, the club disbanded ahead of the 1937-38 season.

CHAMPS : VANCOUVER JOHNSTON NATIONAL STORAGE

1937 Vancouver Johnston National Storage FC : GK Jimmy Waiters; Edward Marsden, Jim Lawrie captain; Horace Heath, Trevor Harvey, Angelo Perri; Johnny Johnston, Leland Morley, Jim Larson, Hugh Greer, Reg Liptrot. Substitutions: James Keith, Les Hunter, James Waring. Manager Doug Brown. Missed Final: Jackie Johnson (injured).

BRITISH COLUMBIA SECTION	PROVINCIAL WINNERS	SCORE	RUNNERS UP
1937-07-10 Vancouver, BC	Vancouver Johnstons W	2-0 L	BC Electric
CONNAUGHT CUP SERIES	**HOME TEAM**	**SCORE**	**AWAY TEAM**
1937-07-19 Calgary, AB	Edmonton Civics L	0-2 W	Vancouver Johnstons
1937-07-20 Calgary, AB	Edmonton Civics L	2-3 W	Vancouver Johnstons
Vancouver won 5-2 on aggregate to eliminate Edmonton in the first round.			
1937-07-22 Winnipeg, MB	United Weston FC W	3-2 L	Vancouver Johnstons
1937-07-24 Winnipeg, MB	United Weston FC L	0-2 W	Vancouver Johnstons
1937-07-26 Winnipeg, MB	United Weston FC L	0-2 W	Vancouver Johnstons
CHALLENGE TROPHY FINAL	**CHAMPIONS**	**SCORE**	**RUNNERS UP**
1937-07-29 Winnipeg, MB	Vancouver Johnstons L	1-3 W	Toronto Ulster United FC
1937-07-31 Winnipeg, MB	Vancouver Johnstons W	3-1 L	Toronto Ulster United FC
1937-08-02 Winnipeg, MB	Vancouver Johnstons W	3-2 L	Toronto Ulster United FC

Vancouver Johnstons won the best-of-three series to capture the Challenge Trophy.
Hero of the Connaught Cup Series : centre forward Swede Larson.

1938 North Shore United FC
FIRST DOMINION CHAMPIONSHIP

10 TO 17 AUGUST 1938 - CARRUTHERS PARK IN WINNIPEG
North Shore beat Timmins for first title

North Shore United FC won the 1938 Dominion of Canada Football Championship after they beat Timmins Dome Mines in an extended Final series that lasted five matches. The two sides were all even after the initial three matches and tied again after the fourth match failed to determine a champion.

The North Vancouver-based club won the series after a 6-2 victory in the last match. Trevor Harvey was the hero of the Final while Mike McManus scored the series-winning goal. Jimmy Spencer (14 goals) and McManus (13 goals) were the top scorers of the interprovincial playdowns.

Three weeks after the Connaught Cup Series, North Shore won the 1938 Province Cup with a 2-0 victory over Vancouver St. Saviours FC.

CHAMPIONS : NORTH SHORE UNITED FC
1938 North Shore United FC : GK John Rabbitt; Tommy Cumming, Bob Harrison captain; Paul Kazoolin, Trevor Harvey, Bill Wolfe; Bill Findler, Jim Larson, Malcolm Mike McManus, Cecil Goodheart, Alex Christie. Substitutions: Basil Robinson, Jack Young. Manager Bill Thomson. Missed last match: Reg Liptrot, Jimmy Spencer (injured). Missed Final: Costain, Ron Hewitt.

BRITISH COLUMBIA SECTION	PROVINCIAL WINNERS	SCORE	RUNNERS UP
1938-07-09 Vancouver, BC	North Shore United FC W	2-0 L	Vancouver St. Andrews
CONNAUGHT CUP SERIES	**HOME TEAM**	**SCORE**	**AWAY TEAM**
1938-07-16 Vancouver, BC	North Shore United FC W	9-2 L	Calgary Callies FC
1938-07-18 Vancouver, BC	North Shore United FC W	11-1 L	Calgary Callies FC
1938-08-02 Winnipeg, MB	United Weston FC W	3-2 L	North Shore United FC
1938-08-04 Winnipeg, MB	United Weston FC D	1-1 D	North Shore United FC
1938-08-06 Winnipeg, MB	United Weston FC L	1-5 W	North Shore United FC
1938-08-08 Winnipeg, MB	United Weston FC L	1-4 W	North Shore United FC
CHALLENGE TROPHY FINAL	**CHAMPIONS**	**SCORE**	**RUNNERS UP**
1938-08-10 Winnipeg, MB	North Shore United FC D	1-1 D	Timmins Dome Mines
1938-08-12 Winnipeg, MB	North Shore United FC L	1-3 W	Timmins Dome Mines
1938-08-13 Winnipeg, MB	North Shore United FC W	1-0 L	Timmins Dome Mines
1938-08-15 Winnipeg, MB	North Shore United FC D	2-2 D	Timmins Dome Mines
1938-08-17 Winnipeg, MB	North Shore United FC W	6-2 L	Timmins Dome Mines

North Shore United FC won the best-of-three series (five matches) to capture the Challenge Trophy. Hero of the Connaught Cup Series : centre half Trevor Harvey.

Vancouver Radials FC
FIRST DOMINION CHAMPIONSHIP

31 JULY TO 5 AUGUST 1939 - CARRUTHERS PARK IN WINNIPEG

Happy Radials captured Dominion title

Vancouver Radials FC won the 1939 Dominion of Canada Football Championship after they beat Montréal Carsteel FC in an extended Final that lasted four matches. Vancouver won the last match 3-1 to lift the Challenge Trophy.

Hap Smith was the hero of the Final and he had two goals and an assist in the last match. Smith scored six goals in nine interprovincial matches, second most in 1939 behind Montréal's Paul Castonguay who scored nine goals in nine interprovincial matches.

Before the Connaught Cup Series, the Radials finished second in the 1938-39 Mainland League standings (behind North Shore United FC) and second in the Province Cup (they lost to St. Saviours FC in the Final).

CHAMPIONS : VANCOUVER RADIALS FC
1939 Vancouver Radials FC : GK Bill Watson; Tommy McKibbin captain, Don Cowan; George West, Eric Camp, Johnny Johnston; Jackie Johnson (George Smith), Johnny McKay, Hap Smith, Hugh Greer, Reg Liptrot. Manager: Harold Till. Missed last match: Norm Kerfoot. Missed Final: Jim Lawrie, Jimmy Waters.

BRITISH COLUMBIA SECTION	PROVINCIAL WINNERS	SCORE	RUNNERS UP
1939-07-08 Vancouver, BC	Vancouver Radials FC L	2-3 W	Vancouver St. Andrews
1939-07-12 Vancouver, BC	Vancouver Radials FC W	2-0 L	Vancouver St. Andrews
1939-07-15 Vancouver, BC	Vancouver Radials FC W	5-1 L	Vancouver St. Andrews
CONNAUGHT CUP SERIES	**HOME TEAM**	**SCORE**	**AWAY TEAM**
1939-07-20 Edmonton, AB	Edmonton Civics L	2-5 W	Vancouver Radials FC
1939-07-22 Edmonton, AB	Edmonton Civics W	3-1 L	Vancouver Radials FC
1939-07-24 Winnipeg, MB	Winnipeg Irish FC D	2-2 D	Vancouver Radials FC
1939-07-26 Winnipeg, MB	Winnipeg Irish FC L	1-2 W	Vancouver Radials FC
1939-07-28 Winnipeg, MB	Winnipeg Irish FC D	3-3 D	Vancouver Radials FC
CHALLENGE TROPHY FINAL	**CHAMPIONS**	**SCORE**	**RUNNERS UP**
1939-07-31 Winnipeg, MB	Vancouver Radials FC D	2-2 D	Montréal Carsteel FC
1939-08-02 Winnipeg, MB	Vancouver Radials FC L	2-3 W	Montréal Carsteel FC
1939-08-04 Winnipeg, MB	Vancouver Radials FC W	2-0 L	Montréal Carsteel FC
1939-08-05 Winnipeg, MB	Vancouver Radials FC W	3-1 L	Montréal Carsteel FC

Vancouver Radials FC won the best-of-three series (four matches) to capture the Challenge Trophy. Hero of the Connaught Cup Series : centre forward Hap Smith.

CANADIAN SOCCER HISTORY
MEN'S AMATEUR FOOTBALL CHAMPIONS

1940s

■ CHALLENGE TROPHY

1946 Toronto Ulster United FC
SECOND DOMINION CHAMPIONSHIP

27-29 AUGUST 1946 - BROADVIEW & OAKVIEW IN TORONTO

Hume scored hat trick in Ulster victory

Toronto Ulster United FC captured the first Dominion of Canada Football Championship in the post-War era after back-to-back victories over Fort William Army, Navy & Air Force. In a best-of-three Final played in Toronto, Ulster United won 3-1 at Broadview and 7-1 at Oakview. Six different Ulster players scored in the Final including Bobby Hume who scored a hat trick in the last match.

Hume was just the second player to score a hat trick in the last match of the Final (after Jock Coulter scored four goals in the 1928 Final).

After six years without a Championship, only three regions took part in the 1946 Dominion series: Ontario, New Ontario and Québec. Across the two rounds, Ulster scored 14 goals in four matches against Montréal Carsteel FC and Fort William AN&AF.

Alongside the interprovincial playdowns, Toronto Ulster United FC finished undefeated in first place in the Ontario Major League standings (12 wins and two draws). In the September playoffs, Ulster posted four more wins, including two against Hamilton Stelco in the Final.

CHAMPIONS : TORONTO ULSTER UNITED FC
1946 Toronto Ulster United FC : GK Bill Breadon; Bill Davison captain, Cy Davies; Paul Hric, Norm Rawley, Archie McDowall; Art Varley, Harry McQueston, Jackie Rudland, Bobby Hume, Jackie Stevenson. Substitutions: Mickey McBride, Don Ross. Manager George Singleton. Missed last match: Johnny Aiken, Frankie Millar. Winners received their 1946 medals in December 1947.

ONTARIO SECTION		HOME TEAM	SCORE	AWAY TEAM
1946-07-10	Toronto, ON	Toronto Wear-Ever FC	1-7	Toronto Ulster United FC
1946-07-10	Toronto, ON	Toronto Ulster United FC	1-1	Toronto Wear-Ever FC
INTERPROVINCIAL PLAYDOWNS		**HOME TEAM**	**SCORE**	**AWAY TEAM**
1946-08-17	Montréal, QC	Montréal Carsteel FC L	0-1 W	Toronto Ulster United FC
1946-08-24	Toronto, ON	Toronto Ulster United FC W	3-1 L	Montréal Carsteel FC
CHALLENGE TROPHY FINAL		**HOME TEAM**	**SCORE**	**AWAY TEAM**
1946-08-27	Toronto, ON	Toronto Ulster United FC W	3-1 L	Fort William AN&AF
1946-08-29	Toronto, ON	Toronto Ulster United FC W	7-1 L	Fort William AN&AF

Toronto Ulster United FC won the best-of-three series to capture the Challenge Trophy.

Vancouver St. Andrews FC
FIRST DOMINION CHAMPIONSHIP 1947

20-22 SEPTEMBER 1947 - CALLISTER PARK IN VANCOUVER

Scots scored nine goals in two wins

Vancouver St. Andrews FC won the 1947 Dominion of Canada Football Championship on their home ground after they beat visiting side Winnipeg Scottish FC. The Vancouver Scots won the best-of-three Final with nine goals scored and back-to-back clean sheets at Callister Park. Don Matheson scored a hat trick in the opener while Frank Ambler scored a goal in that same match plus two more in the second match.

Unfortunately, the Challenge Trophy was still en route to Vancouver when the Final wrapped up, so the trophy wasn't available for presentation on the day that Vancouver clinched the title.

Six regions took part in the 1947 series with British Columbia given a bye straight into the Final. Winnipeg had to beat Fort William in the first round, Edmonton Northside Legion in the second round, and Montréal Carsteel FC in the third round. Defending champions Toronto Ulster United FC were eliminated by Carsteel FC.

Before the interprovincial playdowns, St. Andrews FC won the Mainland Cup in February, clinched the 1946-47 Pacific Coast League championship in May, and won the Province Cup in June. In league play, they scored a record 79 goals in 20 matches with 16 wins and two draws (they won the First Half and Second Half with identical 8-1-1 records).

CHAMPIONS : VANCOUVER ST. ANDREWS FC
1947 Vancouver St. Andrews FC : GK Bobby Newbold; Erling Storness, John Webber; Wes Henderson, Nick Glover, Jackie Jones; Jimmy Greig, Don Matheson, Frank Ambler, Johnny Newbold, Ted Enefer. Substitutions: Cecil Goodheart, George Steele. Manager: Bill Findler Missed last match: Johnny McKay, Dave Simpson. The winners received their medals on 10 January 1948.

BRITISH COLUMBIA SECTION	HOME TEAM	SCORE	AWAY TEAM
1947-07-19 Vancouver, BC	Vancouver St. Andrews FC	W 5-2	L Collingwood
CHALLENGE TROPHY FINAL	**HOME TEAM**	**SCORE**	**AWAY TEAM**
1947-09-20 Vancouver, BC	Vancouver St. Andrews FC	W 5-0	L Winnipeg Scottish FC
1947-09-22 Vancouver, BC	Vancouver St. Andrews FC	W 4-0	L Winnipeg Scottish FC

Vancouver St. Andrews FC won the best-of-three series to capture the Challenge Trophy.

■ CHALLENGE TROPHY

1948 *Montréal Carsteel FC*
FIRST DOMINION CHAMPIONSHIP

7-11 AUGUST 1948 - OAKVIEW & BROADVIEW IN TORONTO

Young Castonguay scored series winner

Montréal Carsteel FC scored three times in the last 45 minutes to wrestle the 1948 Dominion of Canada Football Championship away from the defending champions Vancouver St. Andrews FC. The two sides won a match each before Montréal won the decider 4-3 on Marcel Castonguay's series-winning goal in the 81st minute at Broadview Park in Toronto.

Montréal also had to come from behind to win the opening match when captain Doug McMahon scored both the equaliser and match winner. After Vancouver won the second match, Vancouver held a 3-2 lead in the third match before Montréal's McMahon scored the equaliser and Castonguay scored the winner.

Just 10 days after they won the Dominion title, Carsteel won the 1948 Québec Cup with a 4-0 win over Canadair Falcons. Carsteel won the Meighen Trophy as National League Québec first-place winners in September and then captured the Atholstan Trophy in the October playoffs when they beat Hamilton Westinghouse FC.

CHAMPIONS : MONTRÉAL CARSTEEL FC

1948 Montréal Carsteel FC : GK Jimmy Fleming; Tommy Turley, George White; Dickie Walker, Donnie McLean, Willie Gammon (Bill Grundie); Johnny Sinclair, Andy Menyes, Doug McMahon captain, Bill Chambers, Marcel Castonguay. Manager: Alec Samson. Missed last match: GK Danny Smith, Ginger Anderson, Paul-Émile Castonguay, Jimmy Muir, Charlie Warner. Missed Final: Tommy Harris, Jimmy Haswell, Walter Young.

QUÉBEC SECTION		TEAM	SCORE	TEAM
1948-06-26 Montréal, QC		Montréal Stelco FC	3-5	Montréal Carsteel FC
1948-07-01 Montréal, QC		Montréal Carsteel FC	2-2	Montréal Stelco FC
INTERPROVINCIAL PLAYDOWNS		**HOME TEAM**	**SCORE**	**AWAY TEAM**
1948-07-31 Montréal, QC		Montréal Carsteel FC W	4-1 L	Toronto Greenbacks
1948-08-02 Montréal, QC		Montréal Carsteel FC W	7-1 L	Toronto Greenbacks
CHALLENGE TROPHY FINAL		**RUNNERS UP**	**SCORE**	**CHAMPIONS**
1948-08-07 Toronto, ON		Montréal Carsteel FC W	4-3 L	Vancouver St. Andrews
1948-08-09 Toronto, ON		Montréal Carsteel FC L	1-3 W	Vancouver St. Andrews
1948-08-11 Toronto, ON		Montréal Carsteel FC W	4-3 L	Vancouver St. Andrews

Montréal Carsteel FC won the best-of-three series to capture the Challenge Trophy.

North Shore United FC
SECOND DOMINION CHAMPIONSHIP

1949

6-10 AUGUST 1949 - MEWATA STADIUM IN CALGARY

North Shore captured Dominion title

North Shore United FC returned to the top of Canadian soccer when they beat Hamilton Westinghouse FC in the 1949 Dominion of Canada Football Championship. The North Vancouver club won the best-of-three series with clean sheets recorded by goalkeeper Frank Ashdown in the first and third matches. They won that last match 2-0 with goals scored by Trevor Harvey and Fred Whittaker.

Whittaker scored four of North Shore's seven goals in the Final series. Across two rounds in the interprovincial playdowns, he led all players with 11 goals in five matches, including five goals in the second win over Edmonton North Side Legion in the Western Final.

Before the interprovincial playdowns, North Shore United FC won the Mainland Cup in May, clinched the 1948-49 Pacific Coast League championship in mid June, and then won the Province Cup in late June. They beat Vancouver City FC in a best-of-three British Columbia series to enter the Dominion interprovincial playdowns in July.

CHAMPIONS : NORTH SHORE UNITED FC
1949 North Shore United FC : GK Frank Ashdown; Harry Anderson, Tom Cumming captain; Bill Smith, Alex Reid, Jimmy Spencer; Dave Moyies, Trevor Harvey, Fred Whittaker, Davie Brown, Frank Ambler. Alternates. Dick Acaster, George Beckett, George Gray, Stubby McLean. Manager: Bob Harrison.

BRITISH COLUMBIA SECTION	PROVINCIAL WINNERS	SCORE	RUNNERS UP
1949-07-20 Vancouver, BC	North Shore United FC W	3-2 L	Vancouver City FC
1949-07-23 Vancouver, BC	North Shore United FC L	2-4 W	Vancouver City FC
1949-07-25 Vancouver, BC	North Shore United FC W	4-2 L	Vancouver City FC
INTERPROVINCIAL PLAYDOWNS	**HOME TEAM**	**SCORE**	**AWAY TEAM**
1949-07-30 Edmonton, AB	Edmonton North Side Legion L	0-4 W	North Shore United FC
1949-08-01 Edmonton, AB	Edmonton North Side Legion L	0-9 W	North Shore United FC
CHALLENGE TROPHY FINAL	**CHAMPIONS**	**SCORE**	**RUNNERS UP**
1949-08-06 Calgary, AB	North Shore United FC W	4-0 L	Hamilton Westinghouse
1949-08-08 Calgary, AB	North Shore United FC L	1-2 W	Hamilton Westinghouse
1949-08-10 Calgary, AB	North Shore United FC W	2-0 L	Hamilton Westinghouse

North Shore United FC won the best-of-three series to capture the Challenge Trophy.

CANADIAN SOCCER HISTORY MEN'S AMATEUR FOOTBALL CHAMPIONS

1950s

■ CHALLENGE TROPHY

1950 *Vancouver City FC*
FIRST DOMINION CHAMPIONSHIP

12-14 AUGUST 1950 - CALLISTER PARK IN VANCOUVER

Milligan scored four goals in two wins

Vancouver City FC won the Dominion of Canada Football Championship on their home ground after they beat visiting Winnipeg AN&AF Scottish FC in the best-of-three 1950 Final. The local side scored eight goals in back-to-back wins and Wally Milligan led the way with a brace in each match.

Vancouver City FC reached the interprovincial playdowns after they eliminated the defending Dominion champions North Shore United FC in the British Columbia Final. Denny Rogers was the hero in that match after he scored the 4-3 winning goal in extra time.

Across 10 days in August, Vancouver City FC posted four wins in a row as they beat both Calgary Callies FC and Winnipeg AN&AF Scottish FC.

Before the interprovincial playdowns, Vancouver City FC won the Second Half of the 1949-50 Pacific Coast League season, but they lost the league championship after a playoff with the First Half winners Vancouver St. Andrews FC. Milligan was the league's top scorer with 21 goals after he split the 1949-50 season between Nanaimo City FC and Vancouver City FC.

CHAMPIONS : VANCOUVER CITY FC

1950 Vancouver City FC : GK Bill McAllister; Dick Kenning, Roy Cairns; Red McMillan, Pat Philley, Jack Stanley; Bob Lewis, Denny Rogers, Wally Milligan, Ivan Carr, Gogie Stewart. Substitutions: Terry Brennan, Alex McKay, Alan Sawyer. Manager: Jackie Copland. Missed last match: Jackie Dewhirst.

BRITISH COLUMBIA SECTION	PROVINCIAL WINNERS	SCORE	RUNNERS UP
1950-07-12 Vancouver, BC	Vancouver City FC	W 4-3 L	North Shore United FC
INTERPROVINCIAL PLAYDOWNS	**HOME TEAM**	**SCORE**	**AWAY TEAM**
1950-08-05 Calgary, AB	Calgary Callies FC	L 1-4 W	Vancouver City FC
1950-08-07 Calgary, AB	Calgary Callies FC	L 0-2 W	Vancouver City FC
CHALLENGE TROPHY FINAL	**HOME TEAM**	**SCORE**	**AWAY TEAM**
1950-08-12 Vancouver, BC	Vancouver City FC	W 4-1 L	Winn. AN&AF Scottish
1950-08-14 Vancouver, BC	Vancouver City FC	W 4-0 L	Winn. AN&AF Scottish

Vancouver City FC won the best-of-three series to capture the Challenge Trophy.

Toronto Ulster United FC
THIRD DOMINION CHAMPIONSHIP **1951**

15-18 SEPTEMBER 1951 - WESTMOUNT GROUNDS IN MONTRÉAL

Ulster won their third Dominion title

Toronto Ulster United FC won the 1951 Dominion of Canada Football Championship after they beat 1947 champions Vancouver St. Andrews FC in a best-of-three Final. It was Ulster's second Dominion title in six years and their third title since 1925. They won the 1951 series with a win and two draws at the Westmount Athletic Grounds in Montréal.

Johnny Douglas scored four of Ulster's five goals against Vancouver in the Final. The Scottish-born forward also scored one goal in the Eastern Final against Montréal Italia FC.

Against Vancouver, Douglas scored the 1-1 equaliser in the opener and then both goals in a come-from-behind 2-1 victory two days later. Douglas and Hugh Suttie scored the goals in the last match, a 2-2 draw.

After winning the Dominion title, Toronto Ulster United FC wrapped up their 1951 season in second place in the National League Ontario standings behind Toronto St. Andrews FC.

CHAMPIONS : TORONTO ULSTER UNITED FC

1951 Toronto Ulster United FC : George Anderson; John Gifford, Jack Perrett; Sammy Davidson captain, Phil McKay, Archie McDowall; Jimmy Carnegie, Hugh Suttie, Johnny Douglas, Bobby Kennedy, Jack Long. Alternates: Tommy Smith, Vic Malcolmson. Manager: Johnny Aiken. Missed Final: Alf Davies (injured).

ONTARIO SECTION	HOME TEAM	SCORE		AWAY TEAM
1951-09-01 Hamilton, ON	Hamilton Westinghouse	0-1		Toronto Ulster United FC
1951-09-03 Toronto, ON	Toronto Ulster United FC	2-1		Hamilton Westinghouse
INTERPROVINCIAL PLAYDOWNS	**HOME TEAM**	**SCORE**		**AWAY TEAM**
1951-09-08 Toronto, ON	Toronto Ulster United FC	W 2-1	L	Montréal Italia FC
1951-09-10 Toronto, ON	Toronto Ulster United FC	L 1-2	W	Montréal Italia FC
1951-09-11 Toronto, ON	Toronto Ulster United FC	W 3-0	L	Montréal Italia FC
CHALLENGE TROPHY FINAL	**CHAMPIONS**	**SCORE**		**RUNNERS UP**
1951-09-15 Montréal, QC	Toronto Ulster United FC	D 1-1	D	Vancouver St. Andrews
1951-09-17 Montréal, QC	Toronto Ulster United FC	W 2-1	L	Vancouver St. Andrews
1951-09-18 Montréal, QC	Toronto Ulster United FC	D 2-2	D	Vancouver St. Andrews

Toronto Ulster United FC won the best-of-three series to capture the Challenge Trophy.

– CHALLENGE TROPHY

1952  *Montréal Stelco FC*
FIRST DOMINION CHAMPIONSHIP

1-4 SEPTEMBER 1952 - OSBORNE STADIUM IN WINNIPEG

Goaler Gill backstopped Stelco to title

Montréal Stelco FC won the 1952 Dominion of Canada Football Championship after they beat four-time winners Westminster Royals FC on back-to-back days in Winnipeg. After a 4-2 loss in the opener, Stelco won 3-1 and 2-0 to capture the Challenge Trophy. Goalkeeper Bill Gill was at his best on the last day when he posted the clean sheet.

After Stelco beat former national champions Cancar (previously known as Carsteel) in the Québec section, they beat Toronto Italo-Canadians (later known as Italia) in the first round and then beat United Weston FC in the Eastern Final. On the last day of the Canadian Final, Jim McLachlan set up both goals on corner kicks, the first headed in by Bill McKenna and the second headed in by Johnny Sinclair for the 2-0 win.

Just nine days after winning the Canadian title, Montréal Stelco lost 3-1 to Montréal Vickers in the 1952 Québec Cup. After they finished as runners up in the 1952 National League Québec standings, they won the Bunny Sabbath Trophy as playoff champions.

CHAMPIONS : MONTRÉAL STELCO FC

1952 Montréal Stelco FC : GK Bill Gill; Moe Cockburn, Tommy Gummer; Johnny Sinclair, Gordie Rowlands, Giovanni Serrati; Bob McKenna, Hugh Godley, Bill Whitehead, Willie McKenna, Jim McLachlan. Alternates: Dan Carrigan, Gordier Fraser, Johnny Maxwell, Jimmy Thomas. Managers: Alec Samson and Johnny Hutchinson.

QUÉBEC SECTION	PROVINCIAL WINNERS	SCORE	RUNNERS UP
1952-08-09 Montréal, QC	Montréal Stelco FC	W 3-0 L	Montréal Cancar
INTERPROVINCIAL PLAYDOWNS	**HOME TEAM**	**SCORE**	**AWAY TEAM**
1952-08-16 Montréal, QC	Montréal Stelco FC	W 1-0 L	Toronto Italo-Canadians
1952-08-17 Montréal, QC	Montréal Stelco FC	W 3-0 L	Toronto Italo-Canadians
1952-08-26 Winnipeg, MB	United Weston FC	L 0-1 W	Montréal Stelco FC
1952-08-28 Winnipeg, MB	United Weston FC	L 0-1 W	Montréal Stelco FC
CHALLENGE TROPHY FINAL	**CHAMPIONS**	**SCORE**	**RUNNERS UP**
1952-09-01 Winnipeg, MB	Montréal Stelco FC	L 2-4 W	Westminster Royals FC
1952-09-03 Winnipeg, MB	Montréal Stelco FC	W 3-1 L	Westminster Royals FC
1952-09-04 Winnipeg, MB	Montréal Stelco FC	W 2-0 L	Westminster Royals FC

Montréal Stelco FC won the best-of-three series to capture the Challenge Trophy.

CHALLENGE TROPHY

Westminster Royals FC
FIFTH NATIONAL CHAMPIONSHIP

15-18 AUGUST 1953 - DELORIMIER STADIUM IN MONTRÉAL

Westminster win started second dynasty

Just one year after finishing as runners up in the 1952 Canadian Final, Westminster Royals FC won the Challenge Trophy after a best-of-three series with 1953 hosts Montréal Hakoah FC. Both the first and third matches ended in draws, but New Westminster clinched the series thanks to their 2-0 win in the middle match.

The 1953 Final featured the same two goalkeepers as the 1952 Final, with Bill Gill now on Hakoah. This time, teen goalkeeper Ken Pears was the hero as he conceded just the one goal from a Gump Worsley penalty.

Four months before winning the Canadian title, Westminster Royals FC won the 1952-53 Pacific Coast League championship. In late July before the first round of the interprovincial playdowns, they lost the 1953 Province Cup to Vancouver City FC. In October, they won the Jack Diamond Trophy after they beat the Chicago Falcons in a North America Amateur Championship Final played at Callister Park in Vancouver.

CHAMPIONS : WESTMINSTER ROYALS FC
1953 Westminster Royals FC : GK Ken Pears; Alan Sawyer, Roy Cairns captain; Jack Whent, Jim Foster, Bill Hislop; Errol Crossan, Lex Henderson, Wally Milligan, Jack Stanley, Paul Fabris. Alternates: Ivan Carr, Bob Findler, Dave Guthrie, Sutherland. Manager: Aubrey Sanford. Did not feature in last match: Les Hibbert, John MacKay, Jack Spry.

BRITISH COLUMBIA SECTION	PROVINCIAL WINNERS	SCORE	RUNNERS UP
1953-07-04 Vancouver, BC	Vancouver City FC L	3-5 W	Westminster Royals FC
INTERPROVINCIAL PLAYDOWNS	**HOME TEAM**	**SCORE**	**AWAY TEAM**
1953-08-05 Edmonton, AB	Edmonton North Side Legion L	0-5 W	Westminster Royals FC
1953-08-06 Edmonton, AB	Edmonton North Side Legion L	0-10 W	Westminster Royals FC
1953-08-08 Winnipeg, MB	Winnipeg AN&AF Scottish FC D	1-1 D	Westminster Royals FC
1953-08-10 Winnipeg, MB	Winnipeg AN&AF Scottish FC D	0-0 D	Westminster Royals FC
1953-08-11 Winnipeg, MB	Winnipeg AN&AF Scottish FC L	1-5 W	Westminster Royals FC
CHALLENGE TROPHY FINAL	**HOME TEAM**	**SCORE**	**AWAY TEAM**
1953-08-15 Montréal, QC	Montréal Hakoah FC D	0-0 D	Westminster Royals FC
1953-08-16 Montréal, QC	Montréal Hakoah FC L	0-2 W	Westminster Royals FC
1953-08-18 Montréal, QC	Montréal Hakoah FC D	1-1 D	Westminster Royals FC

New Westminster Royals FC won the best-of-three series to capture the Challenge Trophy.

— CARLING'S RED CAP TROPHY

1954 AN&AF Scottish FC
SECOND NATIONAL CHAMPIONSHIP

28-30 AUGUST 1954 - ALEXANDER PARK IN WINNIPEG

Scots won Canada's new Carling Trophy

Winnipeg Army, Navy & Air Force Scottish FC won the 1954 FA Canada Championship on their home ground after they beat 1949 winners North Shore United FC in two matches. The Winnipeg side won 3-2 in the opener and then 3-0 two days later to clinch the best-of-three series at Alexander Park. Captain George James scored three goals in the series.

As 1954 Championship winners, Winnipeg were presented the new Carling's Red Cap Trophy instead of the old Challenge Trophy.

Across three rounds in the interprovincial playdowns, AN&AF Scottish FC were perfect with six-straight wins at Alexander Park in August. Before the Canadian Final, they beat Port Arthur United in the first round and then Hamilton British Imperials in the Eastern Final.

Five weeks after winning the Canadian title, Winnipeg AN&AF Scottish FC clinched their local First Division title after they beat runners up United Weston FC in early October.

CHAMPIONS : WINNIPEG AN&AF SCOTTISH FC

1954 Winnipeg AN&AF Scottish FC : GK Walter Norget; Fred Herold, George McKay; Johnny Swankie, George James, Bobby Allen; Nestor Bambino, Midge Pennington, Jimmy Pines, Benny Benjaminson, Johnny Murphy. Substitution: Roy Paton. Manager: Charlie Caithness. Did not feature: Allan Donnett, Walter Frood, John Henshelwood, Harry Ings, Jock Todd.

MANITOBA SECTION	PROVINCIAL WINNERS	SCORE	RUNNERS UP
1954-07-17 Winnipeg, MB	Winnipeg AN&AF Scottish FC	W 6-2	L Winnipeg FC Germania
1954-07-24 Winnipeg, MB	Winnipeg AN&AF Scottish FC	W 2-1	L Winnipeg FC Germania
INTERPROVINCIAL PLAYDOWNS	**HOME TEAM**	**SCORE**	**AWAY TEAM**
1954-08-05 Winnipeg, MB	Winnipeg AN&AF Scottish FC	W 9-1	L Port Arthur United
1954-08-07 Winnipeg, MB	Winnipeg AN&AF Scottish FC	W 9-0	L Port Arthur United
1954-08-19 Winnipeg, MB	Winnipeg AN&AF Scottish FC	W 5-2	L Ham. British Imperials
1954-08-20 Winnipeg, MB	Winnipeg AN&AF Scottish FC	W 5-0	L Ham. British Imperials
CARLING'S TROPHY FINAL	**HOME TEAM**	**SCORE**	**AWAY TEAM**
1954-08-28 Winnipeg, MB	Winnipeg AN&AF Scottish FC	W 3-2	L North Shore United FC
1954-08-30 Winnipeg, MB	Winnipeg AN&AF Scottish FC	W 3-0	L North Shore United FC

Winnipeg AN&AF Scottish FC won the best-of-three series to capture the Carling's Red Cap Trophy.

Westminster Royals FC
SIXTH NATIONAL CHAMPIONSHIP

18-21 SEPTEMBER 1955 - FRED HAMILTON & BROADVIEW IN TORONTO

Royals won second title in three years

Westminster Royals FC won their second Canadian title in three years after they beat SA Ukraina Montréal in the 1955 Final at Toronto. The Royals won the best-of-three Final after a win and two draws, edging Ukraina thanks to their 3-1 victory in the series opener.

After the Royals edged Vancouver City in the British Columbia Final, they went on the road to eliminate the Calgary Danish Canadians in the first round and then Winnipeg IPAC in the Western Final. Across seven interprovincial matches in three rounds, the Royals went undefeated with 29 goals scored. Gogie Stewart was the team leader with 11 goals scored in the first two rounds while John Halley was the hero in the Final with three goals scored in the last two matches.

Before the interprovincial playdowns, Westminster Royals FC won the Second Half of the 1954-55 Pacific Coast League schedule, but they lost the championship after they were defeated by Vancouver Firefighters FC in a three-match series.

CHAMPIONS : WESTMINSTER ROYALS FC
1955 Westminster Royals FC : GK Pete Demuynck; Dave Stothard, Alan Sawyer; Les Hibbert, Joe Robbins, Bill Hislop; Paul Fabris, Randy Jenkins, John Halley, Gogie Stewart, Reinhold Oleynik (Harry Price). Manager: Aubrey Sanford. Did not feature in last match: GK Bob Bissett (injured), Roy Cairns (injured), Ivan Carr, Bobby Durante, Jim Foster.

BRITISH COLUMBIA SECTION	PROVINCIAL WINNERS	SCORE	RUNNERS UP
1955-08-27 Vancouver, BC	Westminster Royals FC W	1-0 L	Vancouver City FC
INTERPROVINCIAL PLAYDOWNS	**HOME TEAM**	**SCORE**	**AWAY TEAM**
1955-09-07 Calgary, AB	Calgary Danish Canadians L	1-5 W	Westminster Royals FC
1955-09-08 Calgary, AB	Calgary Danish Canadians L	1-7 W	Westminster Royals FC
1955-09-13 Winnipeg, MB	Winnipeg Institute Provista AC L	1-4 W	Westminster Royals FC
1955-09-14 Winnipeg, MB	Winnipeg Institute Provista AC L	0-7 W	Westminster Royals FC
CARLING'S TROPHY FINAL	**RUNNERS UP**	**SCORE**	**CHAMPIONS**
1955-09-18 Toronto, ON	SA Ukraina Montréal L	1-3 W	Westminster Royals FC
1955-09-19 Toronto, ON	SA Ukraina Montréal D	1-1 D	Westminster Royals FC
1955-09-21 Toronto, ON	SA Ukraina Montréal D	2-2 D	Westminster Royals FC

New Westminster Royals FC won the best-of-three series to capture the Carling's Red Cap Trophy.

CARLING'S RED CAP TROPHY

1956 — Vancouver City FC
SECOND NATIONAL CHAMPIONSHIP

SATURDAY 15 SEPTEMBER 1956 - CALLISTER PARK IN VANCOUVER
Philley scored Hale-Co hat trick in Final

Vancouver City FC, known by their sponsor Hale-Co, won their second Canadian title in seven years after they beat Winnipeg FC Germania in the 1956 Final. Veteran Brian Philley led the way with three goals in the first 17 minutes, then got assists on goals by Art Hughes and Eddie Bak for the 5-1 win at Callister Park in Vancouver.

Philley was just the third player to score a hat trick on the last day of the Final after Jock Coulter in 1928 and Bobby Hume in 1946. Teammate Normie McLeod got the assists on all three goals scored by Philley.

Vancouver City FC beat St. Andrews FC in the British Columbia Final to reach the 1956 interprovincial playdowns, which for the first time ever featured single-match knockout rounds. Vancouver City FC got a bye straight into the Western Final where they beat the Calgary Danish Canadians by four goals at Callister Park. One week later, they won the Canadian Final over FC Germania by the same margin.

Four months before winning the Canadian title, Vancouver City FC won the 1956 Province Cup with a 3-2 victory over Victoria Strathcona. Then at the end of October, they finished second overall in the 1956 Pacific Coast League standings behind league winners Westminster Royals FC.

CHAMPIONS : VANCOUVER CITY FC / HALE-CO FC
1956 Vancouver City FC / Hale-Co FC : GK Ken Pears; Dick Kenning, Jack Cowan; Jack Steele, George Bogdanovich, Bill Logan; Gordon McLeod, Syd Gorrie, Art Hughes, Brian Philley, Normie McLeod. Alternates: Eddie Bak, Robert Bruce, Bill Hislop. Manager: Don Petrie.

BRITISH COLUMBIA SECTION	PROVINCIAL WINNERS	SCORE	RUNNERS UP
1956-09-03 Vancouver, BC	Vancouver Hale-Co FC	W 3-0 L	Vancouver St. Andrews
INTERPROVINCIAL PLAYDOWNS	**HOME TEAM**	**SCORE**	**AWAY TEAM**
1956-09-08 Vancouver, BC	Vancouver Hale-Co FC	W 4-0 L	Calg. Danish Canadians
CARLING'S TROPHY FINAL	**HOME TEAM**	**SCORE**	**AWAY TEAM**
1956-09-15 Vancouver, BC	Vancouver Hale-Co FC	W 5-1 L	Winnipeg FC Germania

Vancouver Hale-Co FC goals were scored by Brian Philley (three), Art Hughes and Eddie Bak.
Hero of the Canadian Final : inside left Brian Philley (three goals and two assists).

SA Ukraina Montréal
FIRST NATIONAL CHAMPIONSHIP

SUNDAY 22 SEPTEMBER 1957 - FAILLON STADIUM IN MONTRÉAL

Ukraina came from behind to win '57 title

Pistol Pete Waskiw scored a goal and got an assist as SA Ukraina Montréal came from behind to capture the 1957 Canada Soccer Football Championship with a 2-1 win over North Shore United FC. Runners up two years earlier in a best-of-three series against the Westminster Royals, Ukraina won the single-match 1957 Final at Stade Faillon in Montréal. Joe Feeney scored the match winner in the 73rd minute while captain Zenon Snylyk was Ukraina's best player.

Ukraina outlasted city rivals Montréal Sparta in the Québec Cup Final to enter the interprovincial playdowns at the end of August. Ukraina needed two replays to win the series. After they beat Halifax 8-2 in the first round, they won 2-0 in the Eastern Final to eliminate the Windsor Corinthians.

Just three weeks after winning the 1957 Canadian Final, Ukraina lost the Montréal National League playoff for the Labatt Cup to league winners Montréal Cantalia FC.

CHAMPIONS : SA UKRAINA MONTRÉAL

1957 SA Ukraina Montréal : GK Jimmy McAuley; Myron Hrycyn, Johnny Ursika; Zenon Snylyk captain, Tony Shapka, Ian McVicar; Alec O'Neill, Joe Feeney, Pete Waskiw, Ostap Steckiw, Johnny Pollock. Alternates: GK Joe Schneider, Johnny Neilson, Robert Resch, Mike Senyk, Johnny Sim, Stefan Szylo.

COUPE DU QUÉBEC FINAL	PROVINCIAL WINNERS	SCORE	RUNNERS UP
1957-08-11 Montréal, QC	SA Ukraina Montréal D	1-1 D	Montréal Sparta
1957-08-17 Montréal, QC	SA Ukraina Montréal D	0-0 D	Montréal Sparta
1957-08-20 Montréal, QC	SA Ukraina Montréal W	2-0 L	Montréal Sparta
INTERPROVINCIAL PLAYDOWNS	**HOME TEAM**	**SCORE**	**AWAY TEAM**
1957-08-31 Halifax, NS	Halifax Shipyards L	2-8 W	SA Ukraina Montréal
1957-09-08 Montréal, QC	SA Ukraina Montréal W	2-0 L	Windsor Corinthians
CARLING'S TROPHY FINAL	**HOME TEAM**	**SCORE**	**AWAY TEAM**
1957-09-22 Montréal, QC	SA Ukraina Montréal W	2-1 L	North Shore United FC

SA Ukraina Montréal goals were scored by Pete Waskiw and Joe Feeney.
Hero of the Canadian Final : captain and right half Zenon Snylyk.

■ CARLING'S RED CAP TROPHY

1958  Westminster Royals FC
SEVENTH NATIONAL CHAMPIONSHIP

SATURDAY 20 SEPTEMBER 1958 - CALLISTER PARK IN VANCOUVER

Westminster won third title in six years

Westminster Royals FC captured their third Canadian title in six years in 1958 after they won 2-0 over visiting Winnipeg AN&AF Scottish FC at Callister Park in Vancouver. Tony Crisp and Art Bennett scored the goals in the second half while goalkeeper Fred Briscoe and his defenders posted the clean sheet.

Pre-War star Dave Turner, who won four Canadian titles with the Royals from 1928 to 1936, congratulated captain Roy "Buster" Cairns for winning his fourth title. Cairns won his first trophy in 1950 with Vancouver City FC before he started winning more trophies on the Royals' second dynasty starting in 1953. Cairns won his fifth title in 1960.

The Royals eliminated the 1956 champions Vancouver City FC in the 1958 British Columbia Final before they eliminated the Lethbridge Bombers in the 1958 Western Final. Tony Crisp scored a hat trick in the Western Final at Lethbridge.

Just one week after the Royals beat Winnipeg for the 1958 Canadian title, Vancouver City FC beat North Shore United to capture the Pacific Coast League championship. The Royals, meanwhile, finished in third place in the summer league standings.

CHAMPIONS : WESTMINSTER ROYALS FC

1958 Westminster Royals FC : GK Fred Briscoe; Bob Shenton, Roy Cairns; Bob Lewis, Alex McKay, Ron Paton; Stu Crossan, Harry Price, Tony Crisp, Eddie Bak, Art Bennett. Alternates: Jim Cowie, Bill Grant, Al Green, Les Hibbert, Bill Ogan, Ernie McLaren, Trevor Swangard. Manager: Cecil Goodheart.

BRITISH COLUMBIA SECTION	PROVINCIAL WINNERS	SCORE	RUNNERS UP
1958-07-19 Vancouver, BC	Vancouver Hale-Co FC L	0-2 W	Westminster Royals FC
INTERPROVINCIAL PLAYDOWNS	**HOME TEAM**	**SCORE**	**AWAY TEAM**
1958-09-06 Lethbridge, AB	Lethbridge Bombers L	0-5 W	Westminster Royals FC
CARLING'S TROPHY FINAL	**HOME TEAM**	**SCORE**	**AWAY TEAM**
1958-09-20 Vancouver, BC	Westminster Royals FC W	2-0 L	Winn. AN&AF Scottish

New Westminster goals in the Final were scored by Tony Crisp and Art Bennett.
Hero of the Canadian Final : left back Roy Cairns.

━━━━━━━━━━━━━━━━━━━━━ CARLING'S RED CAP TROPHY ▬

Canadian Alouettes FC
FIRST NATIONAL CHAMPIONSHIP

SUNDAY 20 SEPTEMBER 1959 - FRED HAMILTON PARK IN TORONTO
Montréal side beat the defending champs
• •

Montréal Canadian Alouettes FC came from behind to win the 1959 Canada Soccer Football Championship over seven-time champions Westminster Royals FC. Down 2-0 after just three minutes, the Canadian Alouettes scored twice before the break and scored once more in the second half to win the 1959 Final 3-2 at Fred Hamilton Park in Toronto. Argentine inside left Osvaldo de Brasi scored the winning goal in the 76th minute.

The Canadian Alouettes reached the interprovincial playdowns after they eliminated Québec Cup winners Lachine in the Québec provincial playdowns for the McKellar Trophy. In the Eastern Final against Ontario's Hamilton Italo-Canadians, the Canadian Alouettes won 4-3 in extra time after the 22-year de Brasi scored all four Montréal goals.

In the Canadian Final, Argentine centre forward Héctor Dadderio initiated the comeback when he scored the first goal and then Scottish outside left Johnny Davidson got the equaliser.

In the ten days after winning the Canadian Final, Montréal won their last three league matches of the 1959 season, but still only finished seventh overall in the National League Ontario-Québec standings. The following season, the Canadian Alouettes were renamed Montréal Concordia FC.

CHAMPIONS : MONTRÉAL CANADIAN ALOUETTES FC
1959 Montréal Canadian Alouettes FC : GK Ruben Lus; William Wilson, George Savage; Norberto Yácono, Bob Mascarelli, Tommy Barett captain; Carlos Bustamante, Antonio Bonezzi, Héctor Dadderio, Osvaldo de Brasi, Johnny Davidson. Manager: Nick Schmidingham.

QUÉBEC / MCKELLAR TROPHY	PROVINCIAL WINNERS	SCORE	RUNNERS UP
1959-08-31 Montréal, QC	Montréal Canadian Alouettes	W 4-1 L	Lachine Rangers
INTERPROVINCIAL PLAYDOWNS	**HOME TEAM**	**SCORE**	**AWAY TEAM**
1959-09-05 Montréal, QC	Montréal Canadian Alouettes	W 4-3 L	Hamilton Italo-Canadian
CARLING'S TROPHY FINAL	**CHAMPIONS**	**SCORE**	**RUNNERS UP**
1959-09-20 Toronto, ON	Montréal Canadian Alouettes	W 3-2 L	Westminster Royals FC

Montréal goals were scored by Héctor Dadderio, Johnny Davidson and Osvaldo de Brasi.

CANADIAN SOCCER HISTORY
MEN'S AMATEUR FOOTBALL CHAMPIONS

1960s

■ CARLING'S RED CAP TROPHY

1960  *Westminster Royals FC*
EIGHTH NATIONAL CHAMPIONSHIP

SUNDAY 23 OCTOBER 1960 - EMPIRE FIELD AT VANCOUVER

New Westminster won record eighth title

Westminster Royals FC won their record eighth Canada Soccer Football Championship in 1960 when they beat Toronto's SC Golden Mile at Empire Stadium in Vancouver. It was the Royals' fourth title in eight years from 1953 to 1960.

Former Rangers FC pro John Woods, who represented Canada on their September tour to the Soviet Union and United Kingdom, scored a brace in both the Western Final against Calgary Kickers and the Canadian Final against Toronto. Gogie Stewart, who was also on that same September tour, had a goal in each of the two matches.

Before the interprovincial playdowns, Westminster Royals FC finished the 1959-60 Pacific Coast League season in third place. After winning the 1960 Canadian Final in October, they posted five-straight league wins to capture the First Half of the 1960-61 Pacific Coast League season. They later won the Second Half and won the 1960-61 championship.

SC Golden Mile, who played in the Toronto & District League, were the first Ontario team to play a competitive match in British Columbia.

CHAMPIONS : WESTMINSTER ROYALS FC

1960 Westminster Royals FC : GK Merv Schweitzer; David Stothard, Roy Cairns; Bob Lewis (captain), Al Green, Ron Paton; Stuart Crossan (Gordon Stewart), John Woods, Brian Philley, Gogie Stewart, Jim Cowie. Manager Jack Spry, Coach Cecil Goodheart. Did not feature: Eddie Bak, Neil Gallagher, Mike Hill, Jack James, Johnny Swan, Richie Valentin, Jack James. Missed Final: Les Fabri (suspended).

BRITISH COLUMBIA SECTION	PROVINCIAL WINNERS	SCORE	RUNNERS UP
1960-07-09 Vancouver, BC	Westminster Royals FC	W 2-0 L	Vancouver Capilano FC
INTERPROVINCIAL PLAYDOWNS	**HOME TEAM**	**SCORE**	**AWAY TEAM**
1960-09-03 Vancouver, BC	Westminster Royals FC	W 4-0 L	Calgary Kickers
CARLING'S TROPHY FINAL	**HOME TEAM**	**SCORE**	**AWAY TEAM**
1960-10-23 Vancouver, BC	Westminster Royals FC	W 4-0 L	SC Golden Mile Toronto

New Westminster goals were scored by John Woods (two), Gogie Stewart and Gordon Stewart. Hero of the Canadian Final : inside right John Woods.

Montréal Concordia FC
SECOND NATIONAL CHAMPIONSHIP

SATURDAY 29 JULY 1961 - FAILLON STADIUM IN MONTRÉAL
Montréal pros won another Canadian title

• •

Montréal Concordia FC, two years earlier known as the Canadian Alouettes, won the 1961 Canada Soccer Football Championship after they scored a 1-0 victory over visiting side Vancouver Firefighters FC. It was the Montréal club's second Canadian title in three years and incidentally the last time a professional side won the Canadian title.

Newspapers couldn't agree which Brazilian scored the match winner, whether it was inside right João Jorge or centre forward Olivio Lacerda.

Concordia FC were a professional club who spent the 1961 season playing in both the National League (against sides from Ontario and Québec) and the International League playing (against clubs from around the world). They were runners up in the Second Section of the International League behind Czechoslovakia's FK Dukla Praha.

On the road to the 1961 Canadian Final, Concordia FC won a National League playoff series, then got past the Eastern Canada Pro League's Toronto Italia FC by default.

CHAMPIONS : MONTRÉAL CONCORDIA FC
1961 Montréal Concordia FC : GK Emilio Svich; Héctor López, Gabrielle de Toni; Károly "Charlie" Horváth, Héctor Marinaro, Tommy Barrett captain; Héctor Dadderio, João Jorge, Olivio Lacerda, Tito Maule, José Sanches. Alternates: Humberto Gambaro, Arpad Kiraly, Steve Stancik. Manager Bill Hevesy, Coach Skënder Perolli.

NATIONAL LEAGUE PLAYDOWNS	HOME TEAM	SCORE	AWAY TEAM
1961-05-12 Toronto, ON	Toronto Ulster United FC	L 0-1 W	Montréal Concordia FC
1961-06-18 Montréal, QC	Montréal Concordia FC	W 4-2 L	Ukraina SA Toronto
1961-06-25 Toronto, ON	Toronto White Eagles	L 0-3 W	Montréal Concordia FC
EASTERN SEMIFINAL	**HOME TEAM**	**SCORE**	**AWAY TEAM**
1961-07-22 By default	Toronto City FC	L x-1 W	Montréal Concordia FC
CARLING'S TROPHY FINAL	**HOME TEAM**	**SCORE**	**AWAY TEAM**
1961-07-29 Montréal, QC	Montréal Concordia FC	W 1-0 L	Vancouver Firefighters

Montréal Concordia FC's lone goal was scored by João Jorge.

CHALLENGE TROPHY

1962  AN&AF Scottish FC
THIRD NATIONAL CHAMPIONSHIP

SATURDAY 22 SEPTEMBER 1962 - ALEXANDER PARK IN WINNIPEG

Teen Schepers scored four goals in Final

Winnipeg Army, Navy and Air Force Scottish FC won the 1962 Canada Soccer Football Championship after a 6-1 victory over visiting side Edmonton Edelweiss FC. Winnipeg teenager Johnny Schepers scored four goals in the second half as the Winnipeg side pulled away for their first Canadian title since 1954.

Schepers was the first teenager to score a hat trick in the Canadian Final and just the second player to score four goals in the Final (after Jock Coulter in 1928). Schepers also got an assist on the opening goal by Hugh Jamieson in the 30th minute.

Only three provinces entered the 1962 competition, with Alberta winners Edelweiss FC beating Saskatchewan's Regina Concordia SC in the first knockout match. Winnipeg then beat Edmonton in the Canadian Final, their only match in the interprovincial playoffs that year. AN&AF Scottish FC qualified for the Canadian Final after they beat FC Germania in the best-of-three Manitoba Cup Final.

Before winning the Canadian Final, Winnipeg AN&AF Scottish FC captured the 1962 Manitoba National League championship after going undefeated through their 12-match schedule (nine wins and three draws).

CHAMPIONS : WINNIPEG AN&AF SCOTTISH FC

1962 Winnipeg AN&AF Scottish FC : GK Johnny Van de Malen; Jim Napier, Keono Mirwaldt; Jimmy Baird, Jimmy Moore, Ben McKinlay; Don McKenzie, John Addison, Johnny Schepers, Hugh Jamieson, Jimmy Murphy. Alternates Dodds, Bob Logan, Fred Stambrook. Manager Charlie Caithness.

MANITOBA CUP FINAL	PROVINCIAL WINNERS	SCORE	RUNNERS UP
1962-08-09 Winnipeg, MB	Winnipeg AN&AF Scottish FC L	1-2 W	Winnipeg FC Germania
1962-08-13 Winnipeg, MB	Winnipeg AN&AF Scottish FC W	4-1 L	Winnipeg FC Germania
1962-08-18 Winnipeg, MB	Winnipeg AN&AF Scottish FC W	3-1 L	Winnipeg FC Germania
CHALLENGE TROPHY FINAL	**HOME TEAM**	**SCORE**	**AWAY TEAM**
1962-09-22 Winnipeg, MB	Winnipeg AN&AF Scottish FC W	6-0 L	Edmonton Edelweiss FC

Winnipeg goals were scored by Hugh Jamieson, Jimmy Murphy and Johnny Schepers (four).
Hero of the Canadian Final : centre forward Johnny Schepers (four goals and one assist).

CHALLENGE TROPHY

Vancouver Columbus FC
FIRST NATIONAL CHAMPIONSHIP

1964

SATURDAY 19 SEPTEMBER 1964 - CALLISTER PARK IN VANCOUVER

Columbus scored four to win first title

Vancouver Columbus FC won their first Canada Soccer Football Championship in 1964 after they beat Sudbury Italia FC by four goals at Callister Park in Vancouver. John Comuzzi, Errol Crossan, Giorgio Zambrano and Carlos Franco scored the goals before captain Steve Djorić accepted the Challenge Trophy from Canada Soccer Football Association President Dave Fryatt.

Columbus FC qualified for the interprovincial playdowns when they beat their rivals and former provincial champions Firefighters FC in the BC Province Cup Final. Three months later, Columbus FC traveled to Edmonton where they needed extra time to eliminate Edmonton Ital Canadians SC in the first round. Back home in Vancouver for the Western Final, Columbus FC won 6-0 on a Barry Ihaksi hat trick as they eliminated Regina Concordia SC to reach the Canadian Final.

Before winning the 1964 Province Cup, Vancouver Columbus FC finished third in the 1963-64 Pacific Coast League standings and were runners up in the Top Star playoffs. League winners Firefighters FC won 2-1 in the playoff Final on 24 May, but then Columbus FC reversed the score exactly one week later for a 2-1 win in the Province Cup.

CHAMPIONS : VANCOUVER COLUMBUS FC
1964 Vancouver Columbus FC : GK Ken Pears on loan (GK Merv Schweitzer); Dan Comuzzi, Eddie Bak on loan; Steve Djorić captain, Gene Vazzoler, John Franco; Barry Ihaksi, Carlos Franco, Giorgio Zambrano (Roy Nosella), John Comuzzi, Errol Crossan. Alternates Dino Massignani, Tony Mazzei, Frank Sealy. Manager Peter Mainardi.

BC PROVINCE CUP FINAL	PROVINCIAL WINNERS	SCORE	RUNNERS UP
1964-05-31 Vancouver, BC	Vancouver Columbus FC W	2-1 L	Vancouver Firefighters
INTERPROVINCIAL PLAYDOWNS	**HOME TEAM**	**SCORE**	**AWAY TEAM**
1964-09-05 Edmonton, AB	Edmonton Ital Canadians SC L	2-3 W	Vancouver Columbus
1964-09-13 Vancouver, BC	Vancouver Columbus FC W	6-0 L	Regina Concordia SC
CHALLENGE TROPHY FINAL	**HOME TEAM**	**SCORE**	**AWAY TEAM**
1964-09-19 Vancouver, BC	Vancouver Columbus FC W	4-0 L	Sudbury Italia FC

Goals were scored by John Comuzzi, Errol Crossan, Giorgio Zambrano and Carlos Franco.

■ CHALLENGE TROPHY

1965 *Vancouver Firefighters*
FIRST NATIONAL CHAMPIONSHIP

SATURDAY 25 SEPTEMBER 1965 - KINSMEN CIVIC IN OSHAWA

Firefighters FC scored five for first title

• •

Vancouver Firefighters FC won their first Canada Soccer Football Championship when they scored five times against the hosts Oshawa Italia FC in the 1965 Canadian Final. Art Hughes (two), Jim Blundell, Louis Trischuk and Tom Millar were the goalscorers while Ken Pears and his defenders posted the clean sheet.

The victory came four years after Firefighters FC lost the 1961 Canadian Final by a single goal to professional side Montréal Concordia FC. Firefighters FC were itching to get back to the Canadian Final, but British Columbia didn't enter the 1962 competition, there was no competition in 1963, and Columbus FC beat Firefighters FC in the 1964 Province Cup.

In 1965, Firefighters beat Columbus FC in the Province Cup, eliminated Edmonton Rangers in the first round of the interprovincial playdowns, and smashed their way past Winnipeg AN&AF Scottish FC in the Western Final.

Before winning the Province Cup, Firefighters FC finished first overall in the 1964-65 Pacific Coast League standings, but they were then eliminated by Columbus FC in the playoff Semifinals. The Firemen got their revenge with a 4-2 victory over Columbus FC in the Province Cup Final.

CHAMPIONS : VANCOUVER FIREFIGHTERS FC

1965 Vancouver Firefighters FC : GK Ken Pears; Bob Mills, Gary Stevens; Greg Arnett, Bob Allen, Eddie Bak; Art Bennett, Tom Millar, Art Hughes captain, Jim Blundell, Louis Trischuk. Three alternates traveled to Oshawa. Manager Doug Greig. Missed Final: Don Boyd (lacrosse playoffs).

BC PROVINCE CUP FINAL	PROVINCIAL WINNERS	SCORE	RUNNERS UP
1965-07-01 Vancouver, BC	Vancouver Firefighters FC	W 4-2 L	Vancouver Columbus FC
INTERPROVINCIAL PLAYDOWNS	**HOME TEAM**	**SCORE**	**AWAY TEAM**
1965-09-04 Edmonton, AB	Edmonton Rangers FC	L 0-2 W	Vancouver Firefighters
1965-09-12 Vancouver, BC	Vancouver Firefighters FC	W 7-0 L	Winn. AN&AF Scottish
CHALLENGE TROPHY FINAL	**HOME TEAM**	**SCORE**	**AWAY TEAM**
1965-09-25 Oshawa, ON	Oshawa Italia FC	L 0-5 W	Vancouver Firefighters

Goals were scored by Art Hughes (two), Jim Blundell, Louis Trischuk and Tom Millar.

British Columbia Selects
ALL-STAR CHAMPIONSHIP WINNERS

1966

SATURDAY 3 SEPTEMBER 1966 - ALEXANDER PARK IN WINNIPEG

Young BC selects won Canadian title

British Columbia won the first Canada Soccer Football Championship staged as an interprovincial all-star tournament designed to identify National Team players. British Columbia won the six-team tournament after a 2-0 victory over Québec in the 1966 Canadian Final.

Including the Canadian Final, British Columbia posted three wins and two draws in five matches over the course of seven days. The competition featured provinces from British Columbia to Québec, but no provinces from the Atlantic region.

Four players co-led the tournament with five goals each: Ike MacKay (British Columbia), Norman Patterson (Québec), Adolf Traweger (Saskatchewan), and Tony Adams (Ontario).

From 14 matches, Canada Soccer directors identified 33 players for the National Team Program. Eight months later, that group assembled in Winnipeg from which 18 players were selected for the National Team ahead of Olympic Qualifiers in June 1967. Canada lost that two-match series by a single goal to Cuba. One month later, Canada finished in fourth place at the Winnipeg 1967 Pan American Games.

CHAMPIONS : BRITISH COLUMBIA SELECTS

1966 British Columbia U-23 squad across tournament : GK Bruce Ballam, GK Allan MacLeod; Colin Atkinson, Enzo Benatto, Jim Berry, Ralph Burkinshaw, Kirby Carter, Neil Ellett, Robbie Goodheart, Harold Hansen, Russ Hillman, Dennis Irwin, Sam Lenarduzzi, Ike MacKay, Gary Thompson, Sergio Zanatta. Head Coach Len Burkinshaw.

CSFA NATIONAL CHAMPIONSHIPS	GROUP WINNERS	SCORE	OPPONENT
1966-08-28 Winnipeg, MB	British Columbia	W 4-1	L Manitoba
1966-08-30 Winnipeg, MB	British Columbia	W 6-0	L Ontario
1966-08-31 Winnipeg, MB	British Columbia	D 1-1	D Manitoba
1966-09-02 Winnipeg, MB	British Columbia	D 1-1	D Ontario
CHALLENGE TROPHY FINAL	**CHAMPIONS**	**SCORE**	**RUNNERS UP**
1966-09-03 Winnipeg, MB	British Columbia	W 2-0	L Québec

British Columbia goals were scored by Enzo Benatto and Ike MacKay.

— CHALLENGE TROPHY —

1967  Toronto Ballymena United
FIRST NATIONAL CHAMPIONSHIP

SATURDAY 30 SEPTEMBER 1967 - MEWATA STADIUM IN CALGARY

Beattie scored Ballymena away winner

Toronto Ballymena United FC scored the only goal of the 1967 Canadian Final when they beat their hosts Calgary Buffalo Kickers FC at Mewata Stadium in Calgary. Northern Irish centre forward Ken Beattie scored the lone goal on a header in the 27th minute to capture the Canada Soccer Football Championship.

Toronto Ballymena United FC opened the interprovincial playdowns with a 5-0 away victory over Verdun Celtic. Ken Beattie, Jack O'Neil (two), Gord McLennan and John Anderson scored the goals. One week later, they beat the visiting St. Lawrence Laurentians in the Eastern Final at Scarborough's Birchmount Stadium. O'Neil and Anderson (two) were the Toronto goalscorers. The Laurentians were the first-ever representatives from the province of Newfoundland & Labrador in the Canada Soccer Football Championship.

Alongside winning the 1967 Canadian title, Toronto Ballymena United FC finished second in the Toronto & District First Division standings behind Toronto Celtic FC. Before the start of the 1968 season, Toronto Ballymena United FC were out of operation when they quit the league.

CHAMPIONS : TORONTO BALLYMENA UNITED FC

1967 Toronto Ballymena United FC : GK Michael Thoma; Jim Sullivan, Bob Armstrong, Angus Denniston, Bob Hamilton captain, Bill Curry, John Anderson, Tony Adams, Ken Beattie, John O'Neil, Jim Falconer. Alternates: Brendan Nesbitt, Eric Smith, Dick Weatherup, Gord McLennan. Manager: Jim McCready.

ONTARIO CUP FINAL		HOME TEAM	SCORE	AWAY TEAM
1967-08-05	Toronto, ON	Toronto Ballymena United	4-2	Oshawa Italia
1967-08-12	Oshawa, ON	Oshawa Italia	0-0	Toronto Ballymena United
INTERPROVINCIAL PLAYDOWNS		**HOME TEAM**	**SCORE**	**AWAY TEAM**
1967-09-16	Verdun, QC	Verdun Celtic L	0-5 W	Toronto Ballymena United
1967-09-23	Scarborough, ON	Toronto Ballymena United W	3-2 L	St. Lawrence Laurentians
CHALLENGE TROPHY FINAL		**HOME TEAM**	**SCORE**	**AWAY TEAM**
1967-09-30	Calgary, AB	Calgary Buffalo Kickers L	0-1 W	Toronto Ballymena United

Toronto's lone goal in the Final was scored by Ken Beattie.

Toronto Royals FC 1968
FIRST NATIONAL CHAMPIONSHIP

SUNDAY 29 SEPTEMBER 1968 - STANLEY PARK IN TORONTO

Toronto Royals beat former champions

Toronto Royals FC captured the 1968 Canada Soccer Football Championship after a 2-1 home victory over 1964 champions Vancouver Columbus FC. Each side scored a goal in the first half before Billy Adolfsen scored the 2-1 match winner from the penalty spot in the 76th minute. Goalkeeper Billy Scott and his defenders posted the clean sheet.

Four weeks before the Canadian Final, Adolfsen was the Toronto hero when he scored the 4-3 match winner in extra time against Lachine Johl Rangers in the 1968 Eastern Final at King George V Park.

Consistently one of the better teams in the Toronto & District League through the 1960s, the Royals added six members from the defunct Ballymena United FC side who won the 1967 Canadian title in Calgary.

During the 1968 season, Toronto Royals FC finished second overall in the Toronto & District League's new Premier Division behind Toronto Rangers Supporters. Just two weeks after winning the Canadian title, the Royals won their fifth British Consols Trophy in eight years after a 2-1 win over Toronto Celtic FC.

CHAMPIONS : TORONTO ROYALS FC

1968 Toronto Royals FC : GK Billy Scott; B. Johnson, Frank McAuley, Ken Beattie, Jim McLuskie, Ron Middler, Tony Adams, John Anderson, Chris Doyle (Jack O'Neil), Steve Mackley, Billy Adolfsen. Alternates: Bob Armstrong, K. Laidlaw, T. Mellow, Dick Weatherup. Head Coach Vair Jackson.

ONTARIO CUP FINAL	HOME TEAM	SCORE	AWAY TEAM
1968-08-10 Oshawa, ON	Oshawa Montini Beavers	0-6	Toronto Royals FC
1968-08-18 Toronto, ON	Toronto Royals FC	5-0	Oshawa Montini Beavers
INTERPROVINCIAL PLAYDOWNS	**TEAM**	**SCORE**	**TEAM**
1968-08-31 St. John's, NL	Halifax-Oland SC L	1-2 W	Toronto Royals FC
1968-09-01 St. John's, NL	Lachine Johl Rangers L	3-4 W	Toronto Royals FC
CHALLENGE TROPHY FINAL	**HOME TEAM**	**SCORE**	**AWAY TEAM**
1968-09-29 Toronto, ON	Toronto Royals FC W	2-1 L	Vancouver Columbus

Toronto's goals in the Final were scored by Chris Doyle and Billy Adolfsen.

■ CHALLENGE TROPHY ■

1969  *Vancouver Columbus FC*
SECOND NATIONAL CHAMPIONSHIP

SUNDAY 28 SEPTEMBER 1969 - SWANGARD STADIUM IN BURNABY
Columbus exploded for 10 goals in Final
● ●

Vancouver Columbus FC won their second Canada Soccer Football Championship in 1969 after they put 10 goals past their visiting opponents SA Ukraina Montréal. It was the largest victory ever in the history of the Canadian Final, albeit it was still a close contest after 45 minutes when the score was just 1-0.

Columbus FC won 5-0 over Calgary Shamrocks in the first round, but they were nearly eliminated by Regina Concordia SC in the Western Final two weeks later. Victor Kodelja saved the day when he scored the 4-3 winner in extra time on a penalty kick. He also got an assist on Vanni Lenarduzzi's 3-3 equaliser in the 88th minute.

Before winning the Province Cup, Vancouver Columbus FC won the 1968-69 Pacific Coast League championship (they set a league record with 19 wins) and the Top Star playoff championship (they beat Firefighters FC in the Final).

One week after winning the 1969 Canadian Final at Swangard Stadium, Columbus FC opened the 1969-70 Pacific Coast League season with a 4-0 victory over the University of British Columbia at Callister Park.

CHAMPIONS : VANCOUVER COLUMBUS FC
1969 Vancouver Columbus FC : GK Peter Greco; Jim Berry, Franco Castellano (Dino Massignani), Sam Lenarduzzi, Gene Vazzoler captain, Bob Hazeldine, Victor Kodelja, Alan Bristowe, Dan Comuzzi (Dan Rosengren), Steve Djorić (Peter Simpson), Sergio Zanatta. Alternates: Vanni Lenarduzzi. Head Coach József Csabai, Manager Peter Mainardi.

BC PROVINCE CUP FINAL	PROVINCIAL WINNERS	SCORE	RUNNERS UP
1969-05-19 Vancouver, BC	Vancouver Columbus FC	W 2-0 L	Vancouver Glenavon
INTERPROVINCIAL PLAYDOWNS	**HOME TEAM**	**SCORE**	**AWAY TEAM**
1969-08-30 Burnaby, BC	Vancouver Columbus FC	W 5-0 L	Calgary Shamrocks
1969-09-14 Vancouver, BC	Vancouver Columbus FC	W 4-3 L	Regina Concordia SC
CHALLENGE TROPHY FINAL	**HOME TEAM**	**SCORE**	**AWAY TEAM**
1969-09-28 Burnaby, BC	Vancouver Columbus FC	W 10-0 L	SA Ukraina Montréal

Goals in the Final were scored by Sam Lenarduzzi (two), Dan Rosengren (two), Jim Berry, Sergio Zanatta (two), Victor Kodelja, and Ukraina on their own goal.

CANADIAN SOCCER HISTORY
MEN'S AMATEUR FOOTBALL CHAMPIONS

1970s

– CHALLENGE TROPHY

1970 Manitoba Soccer Selects
ALL-STAR CHAMPIONSHIP WINNERS

THURSDAY 6 AUGUST 1970 - ALEXANDER PARK IN WINNIPEG
Manitoba Selects won the Canadian title

Manitoba won the second Canada Soccer Football Championship staged as an interprovincial all-star tournament when they beat Québec in the 1970 Canadian Final. Walter McKee scored twice in the second half as Manitoba won 2-1 at Alexander Park in Winnipeg.

The hosts went undefeated across four matches at the eight-team all-star tournament, including a 1-1 draw against British Columbia on the opening day of the tournament. Andy Cooper led Manitoba with five goals while Newfoundland & Labrador's Wils Molloy led the tournament with seven goals.

Just like the interprovincial all-star tournament in 1966, Canada Soccer directors used the 1970 tournament to identify players for the National Team program (which had not been together since the FIFA World Cup Qualifiers in October 1968). Eight months later in April 1971, Canada Head Coach Frank Pike organised Eastern and Western identification camps featuring a mix of amateur players from the Canada Soccer Football Championship alongside other recommendations.

Canada were eliminated by Mexico in 1971 Olympic Qualifiers, then finished in fifth place at the 1971 Pan American Games in Colombia.

CHAMPIONS : MANITOBA SOCCER SELECTS
1970 Manitoba squad across tournament : GK Laszlo Bastyovanszky, GK Detlev Gaul; Gary Batchelor, Horst Bluschke, Andy Cooper, Dusan Drazic, Erick Isaacson, Tom Johnstone, Dave Kerr, Nick McGuire, Frank McKee, Walter McKee, Jim McLees, Steve Meszaros, Billy Newlands, Wolfgang Trauer. Manager Charlie Caithness, Head Coach Jimmy Dunnett.

CSFA NATIONAL CHAMPIONSHIPS	GROUP WINNERS	SCORE	OPPONENT
1970-08-02 Winnipeg, MB	Manitoba D	1-1	D British Columbia
1970-08-04 Winnipeg, MB	Manitoba W	5-0	L Saskatchewan
1970-08-05 Winnipeg, MB	Manitoba W	3-0	L Alberta
CHALLENGE TROPHY FINAL	**CHAMPIONS**	**SCORE**	**RUNNERS UP**
1970-08-06 Winnipeg, MB	Manitoba W	2-1	L Québec

Manitoba's goals in the Final were both scored by Walter McKee.

Eintracht SC Vancouver
FIRST NATIONAL CHAMPIONSHIP

MONDAY 3 OCTOBER 1971 - SWANGARD STADIUM IN BURNABY

Young Arnett scored twice in title win

Eintracht SC won Canada Soccer's 1971 National Championship after they beat the Windsor Maple Leafs at Swangard Stadium in Burnaby. Vancouver's Peter Arnett scored two goals including the match winner before older brother Greg Arnett lifted the Challenge Trophy as team captain.

Eintracht SC won their first interprovincial playoff away at Edmonton with a 6-2 victory over Ital Canadians SC. They won the Western Final one week later when they beat Winnipeg Inter Italia at Alexander Park in Winnipeg. Buzz Parsons was the hero in the Western Final after he scored the 1-0 match winner in extra time.

Before winning the Province Cup, Eintracht SC Vancouver finished fourth overall in the 1970-71 Pacific Coast League standings and were eliminated by the league winners Vancouver Columbus FC in the playoffs.

Just two weeks after winning the Canadian title in October, they lost a one-match Open Cup Final to National League Ontario champions Toronto Croatia National SC.

CHAMPIONS : EINTRACHT SC VANCOUVER

1971 Eintracht SC Vancouver (unknown lineup for the Final): GK Graham Lee, GK Andrew Sall; Greg Arnett captain, Peter Arnett, Adolf Becker, Wilfried Bischof, Wolfgang Bludau, Peter Efrenjon, Manuel Gomes, Rifet Malkoc, Buzz Parsons, Bruce Robertson, Bobby Therien, Gary Thompson, Erwin Walko, Danny Webster. Manager Rolly Skov, Head Coach Steve Djorić.

BC PROVINCE CUP FINAL	PROVINCIAL WINNERS	SCORE	RUNNERS UP
1971-05-23 Burnaby, BC	Eintracht SC Vancouver W	2-0	L Vancouver Paul's Tailor
INTERPROVINCIAL PLAYDOWNS	**HOME TEAM**	**SCORE**	**OPPONENT**
1971-09-12 Edmonton, AB	Edmonton Ital Canadians SC L	2-6	W Eintracht SC Vancouver
CS NATIONAL CHAMPIONSHIP	**SEMIFINALS**	**SCORE**	**OPPONENT**
1971-09-19 Winnipeg, MB	Eintracht SC Vancouver W	1-0	L Winnipeg Ital-Inter
CHALLENGE TROPHY FINAL	**HOME TEAM**	**SCORE**	**AWAY TEAM**
1971-10-03 Burnaby, BC	Eintracht SC Vancouver W	3-1	L Windsor Maple Leafs

Vancouver's goals in the Final were scored by Peter Arnett (two) and Danny Webster.

■ CHALLENGE TROPHY

1972  *Westminster Blues*
NINTH NATIONAL CHAMPIONSHIP

SUNDAY 1 OCTOBER 1972 - YORK STADIUM IN TORONTO

New West won their ninth Canadian title

New Westminster won Canada Soccer's 1972 National Championship after they put three goals past hosts Toronto San Fili in the Canadian Final at York Stadium in Toronto. Metro Gerela, Danny Lomas and Doug Wilson scored the goals while Mike Gilmore and his defenders posted the clean sheet.

It was a record ninth Challenge Trophy for the New Westminster club formerly known as the Royals, who since 1967-68 had used a sponsor name from the Labatt Brewing Company.

Goalkeeper Gilmore posted three successive clean sheets across the interprovincial playdowns in 1972. After a 1-0 win over Edmonton Scottish in the first round, New Westminster won 2-0 over Winnipeg Thistle FC in the Western Final.

Before winning the 1972 Province Cup, New Westminster finished fourth overall in the 1971-72 Pacific Coast League standings before they were eliminated in the playoffs by league winners Victoria West United. The following season, they finished at the top of the 1972-73 standings and won the Top Star Trophy as 1973 playoff champions.

CHAMPIONS : NEW WESTMINSTER BLUES (ROYALS FC)

1972 New Westminster Blues : GK Mike Gilmore; Gary Born, Bill Sinclair; Neil Calver, Jim Irving, Brian Gant; Robbie Goodheart, Steven Rogers, Tom Forrester, Danny Lomas, Metro Gerela. Alternates: Rusty Bruce, Joe Little, Doug Wilson. Manager George Wright, Head Coach Joe Johnson.

BC PROVINCE CUP FINAL	PROVINCIAL WINNERS	SCORE	RUNNERS UP
1972-08-06 Burnaby, BC	New Westminster Blues	W 2-0 L	Burnaby Norburn
INTERPROVINCIAL PLAYDOWNS	**HOME TEAM**	**SCORE**	**AWAY TEAM**
1972-09-02 Burnaby, BC	New Westminster Blues	W 1-0 L	Edmonton Scottish SC
CS NATIONAL CHAMPIONSHIPS	**HOME TEAM**	**SCORE**	**AWAY TEAM**
1972-09-17 Burnaby, BC	New Westminster Blues	W 2-0 L	Winnipeg Thistle FC
CHALLENGE TROPHY FINAL	**HOME TEAM**	**SCORE**	**AWAY TEAM**
1972-10-01 Toronto, ON	Toronto San Fili SC	L 0-3 W	New Westminster Blues

New Westminster's goals in the Final were scored by Metro Gerela, Danny Lomas and Doug Wilson. Most Valuable Player of the National Championship : goalkeeper Mike Gilmore.

— CHALLENGE TROPHY —

Vancouver Firefighters
SECOND NATIONAL CHAMPIONSHIP  1973

MONDAY 3 SEPTEMBER 1973 - KING GEORGE V PARK IN ST. JOHN'S

Firefighters went to other coast for title

Vancouver Firefighters FC traveled all the way to St. John's to capture Canada Soccer's 1973 National Championship, which for the first time was played as a final knockout tournament in one venue across three days. Louis Trischuk and John Haar were the goalscorers while Mike Gilmore and his defenders posted the clean sheet in a 2-0 victory.

Firefighters FC beat Saint John Schooners in the Saturday opener and then St-Viateur Montréal in the Sunday Semifinals before winning Monday's Canadian Final over West Indies United Toronto. The runners up had beaten Calgary Springer Kickers on Saturday and then hosts Holy Cross FC in Sunday's Semifinals. West Indies United were the first team of colour to ever reach the Canadian Final.

Firefighters FC reached the interprovincial playdowns after they upset reigning Canadian champions New Westminster Blues in the 1973 Province Cup Final. Firefighters FC then beat Yukon's first-ever entry the Whitehorse Canucks in the opening round.

CHAMPIONS : VANCOUVER FIREFIGHTERS FC
1973 Vancouver Firefighters FC : GK Mike Gilmore; Al Hardy, Gary Stevens; Glen Hunter, Ken Harris, Bob Sedgwick; Louis Trischuk captain, Steven Rogers, John Haar, Robbie Goodheart, Jim Goodheart. Alternates: Robert Allen, Gill, Dave Hutton, Bill Nicol, Bob Rose, Bob Schwab, Brian Singleton, Gil Tetrault. Head Coach Tony Nowitsky.

BC PROVINCE CUP FINAL	PROVINCIAL WINNERS	SCORE	RUNNERS UP
1973-06-03 Vancouver, BC	Vancouver Firefighters FC	W 3-0	L New Westminster Blues
INTERPROVINCIAL PLAYDOWNS	**PLAYOFF WINNERS**	**SCORE**	**OPPONENT**
1973-08-18 Burnaby, BC	Vancouver Firefighters FC	W 6-1	L Yukon Canucks
CS NATIONAL CHAMPIONSHIP	**FIRST STAGE**	**SCORE**	**OPPONENT**
1973-09-01 St. John's, NL	Vancouver Firefighters FC	W 9-0	L Saint John Schooners
CS NATIONAL CHAMPIONSHIP	**SEMIFINALS**	**SCORE**	**OPPONENT**
1973-09-02 St. John's, NL	Vancouver Firefighters FC	W 2-1	L St-Viateur Montréal
CHALLENGE TROPHY FINAL	**CHAMPIONS**	**SCORE**	**RUNNERS UP**
1973-09-03 St. John's, NL	Vancouver Firefighters FC	W 2-0	L West Indies United

Vancouver's goals in the Final were scored by Louis Trischuk and John Haar.
Most Valuable Player of the National Championship : centre forward John Haar.

■ CHALLENGE TROPHY

1974  *Calgary Springer Kickers*
FIRST NATIONAL CHAMPIONSHIP

SUNDAY 25 AUGUST 1974 - KING GEORGE V PARK IN ST. JOHN'S
Calgary's first Canadian title in 52 years

The Calgary Kickers finally won Canada Soccer's Challenge Trophy after they beat Windsor Italia in the 1974 Canadian Final at King George V Park in St. John's. The former runners up became the first Calgary club in 52 years to win Canada Soccer's National Championship, a feat previously accomplished by Calgary Hillhurst FC in 1922.

The former Western Canada League winners were national runners up in 1967, but lost the Canadian Final at home on a single goal to Toronto Ballymena United FC. This time, Calgary made no mistake as they won 2-1 on a Ray Gannon headed goal in the 54th minute.

This marked the second year in a row that Canada Soccer's National Championship was played in St. John's, albeit this time with only four finalists who played Saturday and Sunday. Before beating Windsor, Calgary squeaked past AS Haïtiana Montréal with a 1-0 victory.

Two months after winning the 1974 Canadian amateur title, Calgary lost a one-match Open Cup Final to National League Ontario champions Toronto Serbian White Eagles.

CHAMPIONS : CALGARY SPRINGER KICKERS FC
1974 Calgary Springer Kickers FC (unknown lineup for the Final) : GK Art Jense; Hefin Aberworth, Yilmas Atas, Kim Blank, George Corrall, Bob Dorey, Oscar Faoro, Ray Gannon, Hugh Hamilton, Harold Hansen, Terry Klappe, Kurt Larsen, Dave Oswald, Adam Rath, Otto Seidel, John Sneddon, Roy Warner. Head Coach Walter Niereisel.

ALBERTA CUP FINAL	HOME TEAM	SCORE	AWAY TEAM
1974-07-21 Calgary, AB	Calgary Kickers	1-x	Edmonton Scottish SC
1974-07-28 Edmonton, AB	Edmonton Scottish SC	3-6	Calgary Springer Kickers
INTERPROVINCIAL PLAYDOWNS	**PLAYOFF WINNERS**	**SCORE**	**AWAY TEAM**
1974-08-17 Calgary, AB	Calgary Springer Kickers W	3-0 L	Vancouver Lobbans FC
CS NATIONAL CHAMPIONSHIPS	**SEMIFINALS**	**SCORE**	**OPPONENT**
1974-08-24 St. John's, NL	Calgary Springer Kickers W	1-0 L	AS Haïtiana Montréal
CHALLENGE TROPHY FINAL	**CHAMPIONS**	**SCORE**	**RUNNERS UP**
1974-08-25 St. John's, NL	Calgary Springer Kickers W	2-1 L	Windsor SS Italia

Calgary's goals in the Final were scored by Yilmas Atas and Ray Gannon.

— CHALLENGE TROPHY ▪

Victoria London Boxing AC
FIRST NATIONAL CHAMPIONSHIP  1975

SUNDAY 24 AUGUST 1975 - MEWATA STADIUM IN CALGARY

Bolitho scored brace for Boxers' title

Victoria's London Boxing AC captured Canada Soccer's 1975 National Championship after they beat the St. Lawrence Laurentians in the Canadian Final at Mewata Stadium in Calgary. Bob Bolitho scored twice and George Pakos scored once as the club from Vancouver Island won 3-1 over the club from Newfoundland & Labrador.

It was a Canadian Final that featured the greatest distance ever between the last two clubs in the National Championship: more than 6,800 kilometres separated the two clubs from Victoria and St. Lawrence.

Victoria reached the interprovincial playdowns after they beat North Shore United in the BC Province Cup. They joined the final four teams in Calgary after they beat Winnipeg Thistle FC in the opening round, then reached the Canadian Final after they beat Edmonton Ital Canadians SC in the Semifinals. The Boxers were the first team from Vancouver Island in 48 years to win Canada Soccer's National Championship.

Before winning the Province Cup, Victoria London Boxing AC won the 1974-75 Vancouver Island League championship.

CHAMPIONS : VICTORIA LONDON BOXING AC
1975 Victoria London Boxing AC : GK Kjeld Brodsgaard; Ken Ross, Ted Reading, Brian Robinson, Howie Anderson, George Pakos; Ron Thompson, Frank Woods, Garnett Moen, Danny Lomas, Bob Bolitho. Alternates: Jan Bentley, Steve Carroll, Ash Douglas, Steve Carroll. Head Coach George Fox.

BC PROVINCE CUP FINAL	PROVINCIAL WINNERS	SCORE	RUNNERS UP
1975-05-12 Burnaby, BC	Victoria London Boxing AC	W 4-1	L North Shore Paul's
INTERPROVINCIAL PLAYDOWNS	**PLAYOFF**	**SCORE**	**OPPONENT**
1975-08-17 Winnipeg, MB	Victoria London Boxing AC	W 3-1	L Winnipeg Thistle FC
CS NATIONAL CHAMPIONSHIP	**SEMIFINALS**	**SCORE**	**OPPONENT**
1975-08-22 Calgary, AB	Victoria London Boxing AC	W 4-1	L Edm. Ital Canadians SC
CHALLENGE TROPHY FINAL	**CHAMPIONS**	**SCORE**	**RUNNERS UP**
1975-08-24 Calgary, AB	Victoria London Boxing AC	W 3-1	L St. Lawrence Laurentians

Victoria's goals in the Final were scored by Bob Bolitho (two) and George Pakos.
Most Valuable Player of the National Championship : outside left Bob Bolitho.

1976 Victoria West FC
FIRST NATIONAL CHAMPIONSHIP

SUNDAY 29 AUGUST 1976 - ALEXANDER PARK IN WINNIPEG

McLaren hat trick led Vic West to title

Victoria West FC kept the Challenge Trophy on Vancouver Island after they won Canada Soccer's 1976 National Championship in Winnipeg, Manitoba. Gary McLaren scored all three Victoria goals as they came from behind to win 3-2 over the hosts Winnipeg Fort Rouge at Alexander Park. McLaren was the fifth player in the history of the competition to score a hat trick on the last day of the Canadian Final.

Victoria reached the interprovincial playdowns after they beat Vancouver Columbus FC in the BC Province Cup. They joined the final four teams in Winnipeg after they beat Regina Concordia SC in the opening round. They reached the Canadian Final after they beat the St. Lawrence Laurentians in the Semifinals on kicks from the penalty mark. In the Canadian Final, McLaren scored the 3-2 match winner in the 75th minute.

Before winning the 1976 BC Province Cup, Victoria West FC finished the 1975-76 Vancouver Island Soccer League season in second place behind the reigning national champions London Boxing AC. In late April, Victoria West FC beat Oak Bay in the local Jackson Cup Final.

CHAMPIONS : VICTORIA WEST FC

1976 Victoria West FC : GK Jim de Goede; Mike Hardy, Greg Mellish; Butch Foster captain, Darryl Hooker, Ralph Anderson; Steve Forslund, John McGuire, Rob Williams, Gary McLaren, Greg Booth. Alternates: Marc Bolli, Eric Jones, Steve Moss, Gord Reading, Waining Lee. Head Coach Doug Hill.

BC PROVINCE CUP FINAL	PROVINCIAL WINNERS	SCORE	RUNNERS UP
1976-05-16 Victoria, BC	Victoria West FC	W 1-0	L Vancouver Columbus
INTERPROVINCIAL PLAYDOWNS	**FIRST STAGE**	**SCORE**	**OPPONENT**
1976-08-14 Vancouver, BC	Victoria West FC	W 3-2	L Regina Concordia
CS NATIONAL CHAMPIONSHIPS	**SEMIFINALS**	**SCORE**	**OPPONENT**
1976-08-28 Winnipeg, MB	Victoria West FC	D 1-1	D St. Lawrence Laurentians

Victoria won 6-5 on kicks from the penalty mark.

CHALLENGE TROPHY FINAL	CHAMPIONS	SCORE	RUNNERS UP
1976-08-29 Winnipeg, MB	Victoria West FC	W 3-2	L Winnipeg Fort Rouge

Victoria's goals in the Final were all scored by Gary McLaren.
Most Valuable Player of the National Championship : Winnipeg's right half Gary Batchelor.

CHALLENGE TROPHY

Vancouver Columbus FC
THIRD NATIONAL CHAMPIONSHIP

1977

SUNDAY 11 SEPTEMBER 1977 - CENTENNIAL FIELD IN ST. LAWRENCE

V. Lenarduzzi scored Columbus winner

Vancouver Columbus FC won their third Canadian title in 14 years after they beat the host St. Lawrence Laurentians at Canada Soccer's 1977 National Championship. Vanni Lenarduzzi was the hero after he scored the match winner in the 69th minute in front of a packed crowd at Centennial Soccer Field. Peter Greco posted the clean sheet.

Columbus FC reached the interprovincial playdowns after they beat the defending national champions Victoria West FC in the 1977 BC Province Cup. Doug Wilson was the hero after he scored the 1-0 match winner in extra time.

Columbus FC then joined the final four teams in Newfoundland after they beat Edmonton Ital Canadians SC in the opening round, then reached the Canadian Final after they beat Toronto Hakoah in the Semifinals on kicks from the penalty mark.

Before winning the Province Cup, Columbus FC won the 1976-77 BC Soccer League title after they finished one point better than runners up New Westminster Blues.

CHAMPIONS : VANCOUVER COLUMBUS FC

1977 Vancouver Columbus FC : GK Peter Greco; Fillipo Rigazzi, Doug Wilson; Colin Atkinson, Gene Vazzoler, Billy McLeod, Ed Arnicans, Jan Prehal, Vanni Lenarduzzi, Norman McLeod, Sergio Zanatta. Alternates: Mike McLeod, Tom Newman. Manager Paul Anthony. Did not travel: Reno Agostinis, Tony Canta, Frank Castilano, Wes McLeod (FIFA World Cup Qualifiers).

BC PROVINCE CUP FINAL	PROVINCIAL WINNERS	SCORE	AWAY TEAM
1977-05-14 Burnaby, BC	Vancouver Columbus FC	W 1-0 L	Victoria West FC
INTERPROVINCIAL PLAYDOWNS	**FIRST STAGE**	**SCORE**	**AWAY TEAM**
1977-08-06 Edmonton, AB	Vancouver Columbus FC	W 3-1 L	Edm. Ital Canadians SC
CS NATIONAL CHAMPIONSHIP	**SEMIFINALS**	**SCORE**	**OPPONENT**
1977-09-10 St. Lawrence, NL	Vancouver Columbus FC	D 1-1 D	Toronto Hakoah

Vancouver won 6-5 on kicks from the penalty mark.

CHALLENGE TROPHY FINAL	CHAMPIONS	SCORE	RUNNERS UP
1977-09-11 St. Lawrence, NL	Vancouver Columbus FC	W 1-0 L	St. Lawrence Laurentians

Vancouver's lone goal in the Final was scored by Vanni Lenarduzzi.

— CHALLENGE TROPHY —

1978  Vancouver Columbus FC
FOURTH NATIONAL CHAMPIONSHIP

SUNDAY 10 SEPTEMBER 1978 - MEMORIAL STADIUM IN KITCHENER

Columbus won their fourth Canadian title

Vancouver Columbus FC were back-to-back national champions after they beat Montréal's Elio Blues at Canada Soccer's 1978 National Championship in Kitchener, Ontario. The four-time winners won 3-1 in the Canadian Final after they scored three times in the first 20 minutes: two goals by MVP Robin Elliott and one goal by Vanni Lenarduzzi.

Columbus FC qualified for the Western Regional playoff after they beat Vancouver Eldorado Glens in the 1978 BC Province Cup. Columbus FC qualified for the National Championship after they beat the Calgary Springer Kickers and they reached the Canadian Final after they beat the St. Lawrence Laurentians. Across two weekends in Edmonton and Kitchener, Elliott led Columbus FC with six goals in six matches.

Before winning the 1978 Province Cup, Vancouver Columbus FC finished second overall in the 1977-78 BC League standings.

CHAMPIONS : VANCOUVER COLUMBUS FC

1978 Vancouver Columbus FC : GK Peter Greco; Fillipo Rigazzi, Doug Wilson; Colin Atkinson, Alan McAvoy, Gene Vazzoler; Elio Ciaccia, Norman McLeod, Vanni Lenarduzzi, Robin Elliot, Sergio Zanatta. Alternates: Joe Cuzzetto, Mike McLeod, GK Hank Polvedore, Ivan Belfiore, Billy McLeod. Head Coach Tony Canta, Manager Paul Anthony.

BC PROVINCE CUP FINAL	PROVINCIAL WINNERS	SCORE	RUNNERS UP
1978-06-04 Vancouver, BC	Vancouver Columbus FC	W 1-0 L	Vanc. Eldorado Glens
INTERPROVINCIAL PLAYDOWNS	**PLAYOFF WINNERS**	**SCORE**	**OPPONENT**
1978-09-01 Edmonton, AB	Vancouver Columbus FC	W 5-1 L	Regina Concordia SC
1978-09-02 Edmonton, AB	Vancouver Columbus FC	W 5-0 L	Charleswood United
1978-09-03 Edmonton, AB	Vancouver Columbus FC	W 3-1 L	Calgary Springer Kickers
CS NATIONAL CHAMPIONSHIP	**FIRST STAGE**	**SCORE**	**OPPONENT**
1978-09-08 Kitchener, ON	Vancouver Columbus FC	L 0-1 W	Elio Blues de Montréal
CS NATIONAL CHAMPIONSHIPS	**SEMIFINALS**	**SCORE**	**OPPONENT**
1978-09-09 Kitchener, ON	Vancouver Columbus FC	W 5-0 L	St. Lawrence Laurentians
CHALLENGE TROPHY FINAL	**CHAMPIONS**	**SCORE**	**RUNNERS UP**
1978-09-10 Kitchener, ON	Vancouver Columbus FC	W 3-1 L	Montréal Elio Blues

Vancouver's goals in the Final were scored by Robin Elliott (two) and Vanni Lenarduzzi.
Most Valuable Player of the National Championship : Robin Elliott.

Victoria West FC
SECOND NATIONAL CHAMPIONSHIP  1979

SUNDAY 16 SEPTEMBER 1979 - ROYAL ATHLETIC PARK IN VICTORIA
Vic West back on top with another title

Victoria West FC scored six times on their home ground to win Canada Soccer's 1979 National Championship at Royal Athletic Park, the club's second Canadian title in just four years. The Vancouver Island-based club swarmed Québec's LaSalle Olympique for a 6-2 win on goals scored by Garnet Moen (two), Steve Forslund (two), John McGuire and Dan Henry.

As hosts, the BC Province Cup winners earned a direct berth into the 1979 National Championship alongside winners from the Western (Winnipeg Tatra SC), Central (LaSalle) and Eastern (Holy Cross FC) playoffs. Victoria West FC had beaten Croatia SC Vancouver in the 1979 Province Cup.

At the National Championship, Victoria beat Holy Cross FC in the opener, eliminated Winnipeg in the Semifinals, and then beat LaSalle in the Canadian Final.

Before winning the 1979 BC Province Cup, Victoria West FC finished the 1978-79 Vancouver Island Soccer League regular season in second place behind former national champions Victoria Athletics (formerly known as Boxing Club AC). In late April, Victoria West FC beat the Athletics for the Price Cup playoff title and beat Prospect Lake for the Jackson Cup.

CHAMPIONS : VICTORIA WEST FC
1979 Victoria West FC : GK Jim de Goede; Waining Lee, Greg Mellish; Butch Foster, Steve Moss, John McGuire, Steve Forslund, Rob Williams, Garnett Moen, Tim Achtzner, Bobby Duncan. Alternates: Jaroslav Hrasky, Danny Henry, Darryl Hooker (injured).

BC PROVINCE CUP FINAL	PROVINCIAL WINNERS	SCORE	RUNNERS UP
1979-06-09 Victoria, BC	Victoria West FC	W 5-0	L Croatia SC Vancouver
CS NATIONAL CHAMPIONSHIP	**PLAYOFF**	**SCORE**	**OPPONENT**
1979-09-14 Victoria, BC	Victoria West FC	W 2-0	L Holy Cross FC
CS NATIONAL CHAMPIONSHIP	**SEMIFINALS**	**SCORE**	**OPPONENT**
1979-09-15 Victoria, BC	Victoria West FC	D 2-2	D Winnipeg Tatra SC
Victoria won on kicks from the penalty mark.			
CHALLENGE TROPHY FINAL	**CHAMPIONS**	**SCORE**	**RUNNERS UP**
1979-09-16 Victoria, BC	Victoria West FC	W 6-2	L LaSalle Olympique SC
Goals were scored by Garnet Moen (two), Steve Forslund (two), John McGuire and Dan Henry.			

CANADIAN SOCCER HISTORY
MEN'S AMATEUR FOOTBALL CHAMPIONS

1980s

■ CHALLENGE TROPHY

1980 Saint John Islanders
FIRST NATIONAL CHAMPIONSHIP

SUNDAY 14 OCTOBER 1980 - ST. MARY'S STADIUM IN HALIFAX

First champions from Atlantic Canada

Saint John Drydock Islanders became the first club from the Atlantic provinces to capture Canada Soccer's National Championship when they beat Ottawa Maple Leaf Almrausch in the 1980 Canadian Final. Adel Bashalani scored first before Derek England scored once in each half for the 3-2 victory at St. Mary's Stadium in Halifax.

Saint John reached the Canadian Final after they upset the defending national champions Victoria West FC in the Semifinals. Bashalani and Malcolm Taylor were the goalscorers in the 2-0 victory while Player of the Match David Harding posted the clean sheet.

Alongside winning the Canadian title, Saint John Drydock Islanders finished as runners up in the 1980 Atlantic Soccer League standings behind Scotia Olympics. Saint John qualified for the interprovincial playdowns after they beat Fredericton Capitals in the New Brunswick provincial championship.

CHAMPIONS : SAINT JOHN DRYDOCK ISLANDERS
1980 Saint John Drydock Islanders : GK David Harding; Ashton, Tony Hawker, Matt Reid Player-Coach, Willie Smith, Docherty, Alaisdar Graham, Jim Kakaletris, Crilly, Malcolm Taylor, Adel Bashalani. Alternates: Derek England, Russell Avis, Pierre El Khoury, Faulds, Tim Hicks, Brian Slaney. Manager John Shephard.

NEW BRUNSWICK CUP FINAL	HOME TEAM	SCORE	AWAY TEAM
1980-08-03 Fredericton, NB	Fredericton Caps	?	Saint John Islanders
1980-08-10 Saint John, NB	Saint John Islanders	?	Fredericton Caps
Saint John won the two-leg series.			
INTERPROVINCIAL PLAYDOWNS	**PLAYOFF WINNERS**	**SCORE**	**TEAM**
1980-08-24 Fredericton, NB	Saint John Islanders	W 4-1 L	St. Lawrence Laurentians
CS NATIONAL CHAMPIONSHIPS	**SEMIFINALS**	**SCORE**	**OPPONENT**
1980-09-12 Halifax, NS	Saint John Islanders	W 2-0 L	Victoria West FC
CHALLENGE TROPHY FINAL	**CHAMPIONS**	**SCORE**	**RUNNERS UP**
1980-09-14 Halifax, NS	Saint John Islanders	W 3-2 L	Maple Leaf Almrausch

Saint John's goals in the Final were scored by Adel Bashalani and Derek England (two).
Most Valuable Player of the National Championship : Derek England.

North York Ciociaro SC
FIRST NATIONAL CHAMPIONSHIP

MONDAY 11 OCTOBER 1981 - GLENMORE PARK IN CALGARY
Ciociaro beat the hosts for their first title

North York Ciociaro SC captured Canada Soccer's National Championship after they beat hosts Calgary Springer Kickers in the 1981 Canadian Final. Tony Desousa and Angelo Gabrielli both scored in the second half as Ciociaro won 2-1 away at Glenmore Park.

North York Ciociaro SC reached the 1981 National Championship after they beat CS Hermès Montréal in the interprovincial playdowns Central Regional Final. In Calgary, Ciociaro reached the Canadian Final after they beat St. John's Holy Cross FC in the Semifinals on a goal scored by Victor Tedesco.

North York Ciociaro SC qualified for the 1981 interprovincial playdowns after they won the 1980 Ontario Cup in Oshawa. Down 2-0 against Hamilton Dundas United, Ciociaro came from behind to win 4-2 on goals scored by Pat Petracca, Ronald Hunte, Mike Bracciale and Beham Abassi.

Ciociaro spent the 1981 season in the Toronto & District League Premier Division.

CHAMPIONS : NORTH YORK CIOCIARO SC
1981 North York Ciociaro SC (unknown lineup for the Final) : Behnam Abbassi, Nador Afoussi, Joe Berta, Joe Camevalo, Tony De Sousa, Angelo Gabrielli captain, Sandro Gennara, Frank Gugliolmelli, Tony Lizzi, Joe Pellegrino, Pat Petracca, Mike Pirone, Dave Poroc, Nick Silvieri, Victor Tedesco, Nunzio Teofilo.

1980 ONTARIO CUP FINAL	PROVINCIAL WINNERS	SCORE	RUNNERS UP
1980-09-28 Oshawa, ON	North York Ciociaro SC	W 4-2 L	Hamilton Dundas United
1981 INTERPROVINCIAL PLAYDOWNS	**HOME TEAM**	**SCORE**	**AWAY TEAM**
1981-09-27 Montréal, QC	CS Hermès Montréal	L W	North York Ciociaro SC
CS NATIONAL CHAMPIONSHIP	**SEMIFINALS**	**SCORE**	**OPPONENT**
1981-10-09 Calgary, AB	North York Ciociaro SC	W 1-0 L	Holy Cross FC
CHALLENGE TROPHY FINAL	**CHAMPIONS**	**SCORE**	**RUNNERS UP**
1981-10-11 Calgary, AB	North York Ciociaro SC	W 2-1 L	Calgary Springer Kickers

North York's goals in the Final were scored by Tony Desousa and Angelo Gabrielli.

■ CHALLENGE TROPHY

1982  Victoria West FC
THIRD NATIONAL CHAMPIONSHIP

SUNDAY 10 OCTOBER 1982 - FAIRVIEW FIELD IN SASKATOON
Vic West the best in Canada for third time

Victoria West FC won their third Canadian title in seven years when they defeated the hosts Saskatoon United SC at Canada Soccer's 1982 National Championship. Rob Williams, Steve Forslund, Dan Henry and Howie Kirk scored the goals while goalkeeper Jim de Goede posted the clean sheet in a 4-0 victory at Fairview Field.

Victoria West FC reached the 1982 National Championship after they eliminated Calgary Springer Kickers (the 1981 national runners up) and Winnipeg Tatra SC at the Western regional playoffs in Winnipeg. They reached the Canadian Final after they beat the Kitchener Olympics by three goals in the Semifinals. Henry (two) and Williams were the goalscorers in the 3-0 victory over Kitchener.

Before winning the 1982 BC Province Cup, Victoria West FC finished the 1981-82 Vancouver Island Soccer League season in second place behind Victoria Athletics. In late April, Victoria West FC beat the University of Victoria for the Jackson Cup. Victoria reached the BC Province Cup after they beat Kamloops Furtown in the provincial Semifinals.

CHAMPIONS : VICTORIA WEST FC
1982 Victoria West FC (unknown lineup for the Final) : GK Jim de Goede; Tim Achtzner, Paul Askew, Steve Forslund, Butch Foster, Dan Henry, Howie Kirk, Waining Lee, Ike MacKay, John McGuire, Gary McLaren, Dallas Moen, Steve Moss, Robbie Wallace, Rob Williams. Head Coach Bob English.

BC PROVINCE CUP FINAL	PROVINCIAL WINNERS	SCORE	RUNNERS UP
1982-05-16 Victoria, BC	Victoria West FC	W 1-0 L	Croatia SC Vancouver
INTERPROVINCIAL PLAYDOWNS	**PLAYOFF WINNERS**	**SCORE**	**OPPONENT**
1982-09-24 Winnipeg, MB	Victoria West FC	D 0-0 D	Calgary Springer Kickers
Victoria West FC won 4-1 on kicks from the penalty mark.			
1982-09-25 Winnipeg, MB	Victoria West FC	W 2-1 L	Winnipeg Tatra SC
CS NATIONAL CHAMPIONSHIPS	**SEMIFINALS**	**SCORE**	**OPPONENT**
1982-10-08 Saskatoon, SK	Victoria West FC	W 3-0 L	Kitchener Olympics
CHALLENGE TROPHY FINAL	**CHAMPIONS**	**SCORE**	**RUNNERS UP**
1982-10-10 Saskatoon, SK	Victoria West FC	W 4-0 L	Saskatoon United SC
Goals in the Final were scored by Rob Williams, Steve Forslund, Dan Henry and Howie Kirk.			

Vancouver Firefighters
THIRD NATIONAL CHAMPIONSHIP  **1983**

MONDAY 10 OCTOBER 1983 - FORT WILLIAM STADIUM IN THUNDER BAY
Firemen went back on top with third title

• •

Vancouver Firefighters FC captured Canada Soccer's 1983 National Championships after they beat CNSC Windsor Croatia with a 2-1 victory in the Canadian Final. Vancouver scored twice on scrambles in the 72nd and 73rd minutes at Fort William Stadium in Thunder Bay, Ontario.

Reg Newmark was named the Most Valuable Player of the National Championships after he scored in both the Semifinals (a 2-1 win over Montréal Elio Blues) and Canadian Final. Greg Grieve scored the winner against Montréal while Jamie Buchanan scored the opener against Windsor.

The Firefighters reached the National Championships after they beat Regina Concordia SC in the Western Regional Final.

Before winning the 1983 BC Province Cup, Vancouver Firefighters FC won the 1982-83 Metro Soccer League title and the 1983 Imperial Cup. The Firemen reached the BC Province Cup after they beat the Richmond Canadians in the provincial Semifinals.

CHAMPIONS : VANCOUVER FIREFIGHTERS FC
1983 Vancouver Firefighters FC (unknown lineup for the Final) : Jamie Buchanan, Arthur Coombes, Marty Etheridge, Tom Foss, Kirby Graeme, Greg Grieve, Harold Hansen, Jay Johnstone, John Kveton, Mike McLeod, Norman McLeod, Reg Newark, John Parker, Gord Quilty, Dave Rosenlund, Wilson. Head Coach John Haar, Team Manager Bill Sinclair.

BC PROVINCE CUP FINAL	PROVINCIAL WINNERS	SCORE	RUNNERS UP
1983-05-15 North Vancouver, BC	Vancouver Firefighters FC	W 3-1 L	University of Victoria
INTERPROVINCIAL PLAYDOWNS	**PLAYOFF WINNERS**	**SCORE**	**OPPONENT**
1983-09-16 Calgary, AB	Vancouver Firefighters FC	W 4-2 L	Lethbridge Royals
1983-09-18 Calgary, AB	Vancouver Firefighters FC	W 3-0 L	Regina Concordia
CS NATIONAL CHAMPIONSHIPS	**SEMIFINALS**	**SCORE**	**OPPONENT**
1983-10-08 Thunder Bay, ON	Vancouver Firefighters FC	W 2-1 L	Elio Blues de Montréal
CHALLENGE TROPHY FINAL	**CHAMPIONS**	**SCORE**	**RUNNERS UP**
1983-10-10 Thunder Bay, ON	Vancouver Firefighters FC	W 2-1 L	CNSC Windsor Croatia

Vancouver's goals in the Final were scored by Jaime Buchanan and Reg Newmark.
Most Valuable Player of the National Championships : Reg Newmark.

1984  Victoria West FC
FOURTH NATIONAL CHAMPIONSHIP

SUNDAY 7 OCTOBER 1984 - ROYAL ATHLETIC PARK IN VICTORIA

Vic West won fourth title in nine years

Victoria West FC won their fourth Challenge Trophy in nine years when they won Canada Soccer's 1984 National Championships at Royal Athletic Park on Vancouver Island. It was the second time Vic West won the Canadian title in their home city and this time it took a second-half goal by Dallas Moen to clinch a 1-0 victory over Hamilton's Dundas United.

Alex Hylan presented the Challenge Trophy to Victoria captain John McGuire, one of six four-time winners on the squad alongside Jim de Goede, Steve Forslund, Butch Foster, Steve Moss and Rob Williams.

As hosts, the BC Province Cup winners earned a direct berth into the 1984 National Championships alongside winners from the Western (Edmonton Ital Canadians SC), Central (Dundas United) and Eastern (Dartmouth United SC) playoffs. Victoria West FC had beaten Kamloops Merchants in the BC Province Cup.

Before winning the 1984 BC Province Cup, Victoria West FC finished first in the Vancouver Island League Southern Conference, but they lost the league title after Northern Conference winners Nanaimo City FC beat them in a playoff. Victoria then beat Nanaimo in both the Jackson Cup Final and the Island playoff to qualify for the provincial championship.

CHAMPIONS : VICTORIA WEST FC

1984 Victoria West FC (unknown lineup for the Final) : 1 GK Jim de Goede; 2 Robbie Wallace, 3 Gary McLaren, 4 Butch Foster player-coach, 5 Steve Moss, 6 John McGuire, 7 Steve Forslund, 8 Bobby Mackie, 9 Rob Williams, 10 Dan Henry, 11 Pat Smith, 12 Paul Askew, 14 Yosu Iruretagoyena, 15 Tim Achtzner, 16 Ike MacKay, 17 Clarence Duits, 19 Dallas Moen.

BC PROVINCE CUP FINAL	PROVINCIAL WINNERS	SCORE	RUNNERS UP
1984-05-13 North Vancouver, BC	Victoria West FC	W 3-0 L	Kamloops Merchants
CS NATIONAL CHAMPIONSHIPS	**SEMIFINALS**	**SCORE**	**OPPONENT**
1984-10-05 Victoria, BC	Victoria West FC	W 1-0 L	Edm. Ital Canadians SC
CHALLENGE TROPHY FINAL	**CHAMPIONS**	**SCORE**	**RUNNERS UP**
1984-10-07 Victoria, BC	Victoria West FC	W 1-0 L	Hamilton Dundas United

Victoria West FC's lone goal in the Final was scored by Dallas Moen.
Most Valuable Player of the National Championships : Jim de Goede.

Croatia SC Vancouver
FIRST NATIONAL CHAMPIONSHIP

MONDAY 14 OCTOBER 1985 - CLARKE FIELD IN EDMONTON
Kekec scored twice as Croatia won title

Croatia SC Vancouver captured Canada Soccer's 1985 National Championships after they beat Montréal's Elio Blues in the Canadian Final. Russel Kekec (two) and Skip Radbourne scored the goals while Brian Kennedy posted the clean sheet for a 3-0 win at Clarke Field in Edmonton.

At the National Championships, Vancouver won their group after they posted back-to-back wins over the Moncton Rovers and the hosts Edmonton Ital Canadians. In their 6-0 win over Moncton, Lui Miljanovic scored four times. In their 2-1 win over Edmonton the following day, goalkeeper Kennedy amazingly scored the opening goal after his long goal kick got carried by a strong wind all the way into the opponent's goal.

Croatia SC qualified for the National Championships with a 3-0 victory over NorVan ANAF #45 in the 1985 BC Province Cup. Peter Stipancik, Rudi Gasparac and Kekec were the Croatia SC goalscorers.

Before winning the Canadian title, Croatia SC Vancouver finished first overall in the 1985 Pacific Coast Summer League after going undefeated across the 12-match schedule (eight wins and four draws).

CHAMPIONS : CROATIA SC VANCOUVER
1985 Croatia SC Vancouver (unknown lineup for the Final) : GK Gord Ackerman, GK Brian Kennedy; Dennis Bralic, John Gasparac, Rudi Gasparac, Eric Jones, Russell Kekec, Joe McQuade, Mark McQueen, Lui Miljanovic, Mike Milkovic, Joe Pesht, Skip Radbourne, Darren Schultz, Garry Wilson, Joe Zlomislic, Steve Zlomislic. Head Coach Peter Stipancik.

BC PROVINCE CUP FINAL	PROVINCIAL WINNERS	SCORE	RUNNERS UP
1985-05-12 North Vancouver, BC	Croatia SC Vancouver	W 3-0	L NorVan ANAF
CS NATIONAL CHAMPIONSHIPS	**GROUP WINNERS**	**SCORE**	**OPPONENT**
1985-10-12 Edmonton, AB	Croatia SC Vancouver	W 6-0	L Moncton Rovers
1985-10-13 Edmonton, AB	Croatia SC Vancouver	W 2-1	L Edm. Ital Canadians SC
CHALLENGE TROPHY FINAL	**CHAMPIONS**	**SCORE**	**RUNNERS UP**
1985-10-14 Edmonton, AB	Croatia SC Vancouver	W 3-0	L Elio Blues de Montréal

Vancouver's goals in the Final were scored by Russel Kekec (two) and Skip Radbourne.

■ CHALLENGE TROPHY

1986 *Hamilton Steelers SC*
FIRST NATIONAL CHAMPIONSHIP

MONDAY 13 OCTOBER 1986 - BISHOP'S UNIVERSITY IN SHERBROOKE
Hamilton's Johnstone scored late winner

Hamilton Steelers SC captured Canada Soccer's 1986 National Championships in Sherbrooke after they beat the reigning champions Croatia SC Vancouver in the Canadian Final. Billy Johnstone was the hero after he scored the 1-0 winner late in added time.

The Steelers reached the National Championships after they beat Prince Albert Celtic in the interprovincial playdowns. In the final tournament in October, they won their group after back-to-back wins against CS Dollard-des-Ormeaux and Edmonton Ital Canadians SC.

The Steelers beat league rivals Hamilton Dundas United in the 1986 Ontario Cup, the Ontario Inter-City League, and the Ontario Inter-City League playoffs.

After winning the 1986 Canadian amateur title, the Steelers joined the newly-established professional Canadian Soccer League for the 1987 season. As a professional team, they finished second in the 1987 regular season and finished as runners up in the playoffs behind the Calgary Kickers.

CHAMPIONS : HAMILTON STEELERS SC
1986 Hamilton Steelers SC : GK Bryan Rosenfeld; Billy Johnstone, Gary Morrow, John Di Pasquale, Steve Hill, Lucio Ianiero, Kevin Keenan, Lajos Nagy, Gamal El Shaarawi, Larry Peto, Alastair Love. Alternates: Gary Hay, Colin Samuels, David Tennant, Lino Tomasetti. Head Coach Kevin Grant.

ONTARIO CUP FINAL	PROVINCIAL WINNERS	SCORE	RUNNERS UP
1986-09-13 Burlington, ON	Hamilton Steelers SC	W 2-0 L	Hamilton Dundas United
INTERPROVINCIAL PLAYDOWNS	**HOME TEAM**	**SCORE**	**AWAY TEAM**
1986-09-20 Prince Albert, SK	Prince Albert Celtic	L 0-4 W	Hamilton Steelers SC
CS NATIONAL CHAMPIONSHIPS	**GROUP WINNERS**	**SCORE**	**OPPONENT**
1986-10-10 Sherbrooke, QC	Hamilton Steelers SC	W 0-1 L	Dollard-des-Ormeaux
1986-10-11 Windsor, QC	Hamilton Steelers SC	W 1-2 L	Edm. Ital Canadians SC
CHALLENGE TROPHY FINAL	**CHAMPIONS**	**SCORE**	**RUNNERS UP**
1986-10-13 Sherbrooke, QC	Hamilton Steelers SC	W 1-0 L	Croatia SC Vancouver

Hamilton's lone goal in the Final was scored by Billy Johnstone.

CHALLENGE TROPHY

Winnipeg Lucania SC
FIRST NATIONAL CHAMPIONSHIP  1987

MONDAY 12 OCTOBER 1987 - UNIVERSITY OF MANITOBA IN WINNIPEG

Methot scored Lucania match winner

Winnipeg Lucania SC captured Canada Soccer's 1987 National Championships at home when they beat the New Westminster Queens Park Rangers on a single goal. Kevin Methot was the Winnipeg hero after he scored the only goal of the Canadian Final on a free kick in the seventh minute of the first half. Goalkeeper Steve Hooper and his defenders posted the clean sheet.

At the National Championships, Lucania were Group A winners with three points after a scoreless draw with Scarborough Azzurri and then a 2-1 win over Dartmouth United. After a day's rest, they beat the Group B winners in the Canadian Final.

Before winning the 1987 National Championships, Winnipeg Lucania SC beat local rivals Micalense in the three-match Manitoba Cup Final. Methot scored four goals in the deciding match, a 7-0 victory for the club's historic first Manitoba Cup provincial title.

CHAMPIONS : WINNIPEG LUCANIA SC
1987 Winnipeg Lucania SC (unknown lineup for the Final) : GK Steve Hooper; Robert Albo, Kevin Antonio, John Baillie, Alex Bustos, Dave Dulko, Mark Edwards, Bill Elzard, Keith Ferbers, Chris Harris, Kevin Methot, Marno Olafson, Doug Reimer, Abe Rempel, Venni Sartor, Rob Watson. Head Coach Archie Kane.

ONTARIO CUP FINAL	PROVINCIAL WINNERS	SCORE		RUNNERS UP
1987-09-13 Winnipeg, MB	Winnipeg Lucania SC	D 1-1	D	Winnipeg Micalense
Winnipeg Micalense won first match 5-4 on kicks from the penalty mark.				
1987-09-15 Winnipeg, MB	Winnipeg Lucania SC	W 1-0	L	Winnipeg Micalense
1987-09-20 Winnipeg, MB	Winnipeg Lucania SC	W 7-0	L	Winnipeg Micalense
Winnipeg Lucania SC won the best-of-three series for the Manitoba Cup.				
CS NATIONAL CHAMPIONSHIPS	**GROUP WINNERS**	**SCORE**		**OPPONENT**
1987-10-09 Winnipeg, MB	Winnipeg Lucania SC	D 0-0	D	Scarborough Azzurri SC
1987-10-10 Winnipeg, MB	Winnipeg Lucania SC	W 2-1	L	Dartmouth United
CHALLENGE TROPHY FINAL	**CHAMPIONS**	**SCORE**		**RUNNERS UP**
1987-10-12 Winnipeg, MB	Winnipeg Lucania SC	W 1-0	L	New Westminster QPR
Winnipeg's lone goal in the Final was scored by Kevin Methot.				

■ CHALLENGE TROPHY

1988 Holy Cross FC
FIRST NATIONAL CHAMPIONSHIP

MONDAY 10 OCTOBER 1988 - UMEA WEST FIELD IN SASKATOON
First Canadian title for Newfoundland

Holy Cross FC became the first Newfoundland & Labrador team to capture Canada Soccer's National Championships when they beat Edmonton Ital Canadians SC in the 1988 Canadian Final at Saskatoon. Dick Power and Gus Richards were the goalscorers while Bob O'Leary posted the clean sheet in the 2-0 victory.

The St. John's-based club reached the Canadian Final after they won their group with back-to-back wins and eight goals scored. They won 5-0 over the University of Saskatchewan and 3-0 over Winnipeg Italia SC. Gary Breen scored a hat trick in their first win and scored again in their second win.

Before winning the National Championships, Holy Cross FC beat Lawn Shamrocks for the Newfoundland & Labrador provincial championship in August. It was their sixth provincial title in eight years and their ninth provincial title all time. From there, Holy Cross FC qualified for the 1988 National Championships after they won 3-1 over Dartmouth United SC at the Atlantic Championship in St. John's.

CHAMPIONS : ST. JOHN'S HOLY CROSS FC
1988 St. John's Holy Cross FC (unknown lineup for the Final) : GK Bob O'Leary; A.J. Breen, Bill Breen, Bob Breen, Gary Breen, John Breen, Shawn Browne, George Joyce, Dean Mullett, Paul Mullett, Tony Mullett, Barry Pearcey, Norbert Power, Bernard Reddy, Gus Richards, Daryl Smith, Bob Thompson, Bruce Tobin. Coaches Gerry Reddy and Brian Murphy, Team Manager Brian Tobin.

NEWFOUNDLAND & LABRADOR FINAL	PROVINCIAL	SCORE	OPPONENT
1988-08-21 St. Lawrence, NL	Holy Cross FC	W 2-1	L Lawn Shamrocks
INTERPROVINCIAL PLAYDOWNS	**PLAYOFF WINNERS**	**SCORE**	**OPPONENT**
1988-09-03 St. John's, NL	Holy Cross FC	W 2-1	L Charlottetown
1988-09-05 St. John's, NL	Holy Cross FC	W 3-1	L Dartmouth United SC
CS NATIONAL CHAMPIONSHIPS	**GROUP WINNERS**	**SCORE**	**OPPONENT**
1988-10-08 Saskatoon, SK	Holy Cross FC	W 5-0	L U. of Saskatchewan
1988-10-09 Saskatoon, SK	Holy Cross FC	W 3-0	L Winnipeg Italia SC
CHALLENGE TROPHY FINAL	**CHAMPIONS**	**SCORE**	**RUNNERS UP**
1988-10-10 Saskatoon, SK	Holy Cross FC	W 2-0	L Edm. Ital Canadians SC

Holy Cross FC's goals in the Final were scored by Norbert "Dick" Power and Gus Richards.

■ CHALLENGE TROPHY ■

Scarborough Azzurri SC
FIRST NATIONAL CHAMPIONSHIP 1989

MONDAY 9 OCTOBER 1989 - KING GEORGE V PARK IN ST. JOHN'S

Scarborough came from behind to win

Scarborough Azzurri SC came from behind twice to win Canada Soccer's 1989 National Championships when they beat the hosts and defending champions Holy Cross FC in the Canadian Final. Dino Mastrogiaosis scored the 1-1 goal in the 41st minute, Bart Cramarossa scored the 2-2 equaliser in the 69th minute, and George Argyropoulos scored the 3-2 match winner in the 84th minute.

Goalkeeper Greg Tassino, who featured in the second half of the Final, was named the Most Valuable Player of the National Championships. Scarborough reached the Final after they won their group with two more goals scored than Edmonton Ital Canadians (they were both tied with three points and +2 goals difference from two group matches).

Alongside their wins in the Ontario Cup and National Championships, Scarborough Azzurri SC finished as runners up in the Ontario Soccer League behind winners Hamilton Dundas United.

CHAMPIONS : SCARBOROUGH AZZURRI SC

1989 Scarborough Azzurri SC (unknown lineup for the Final) : GK Steve Hatzinikov, GK Greg Tassino; George Argyropoulos, Bart Cramarossa, Greg Dachanz, Keith Deaskeu, Ken Dodd, Patrick Edmund, Mark Gibbs, Rick Harrison, Doug Irriss, Mike Madonça, Dino Mastrogianis, Peter Norde, Colin Pryce, Derck Tomassis, Dereck Wilson, Nick Bontis, John Williams. Head Coach Tony Lupinacci, Assistant John Stouropoulos.

ONTARIO CUP FINAL	PROVINCIAL WINNERS	SCORE		RUNNERS UP
1989-09-18 Burlington, ON	Scarborough Azzurri SC	W 2-1	L	Hamilton Star
INTERPROVINCIAL PLAYDOWNS	**PLAYOFF WINNERS**	**SCORE**		**OPPONENT**
1989-09-22 North York, ON	Scarborough Azzurri SC	W 5-1	L	Hampstead SC
1989-09-24 North York, ON	Scarborough Azzurri SC	W 2-1	L	Saskatoon United
CS NATIONAL CHAMPIONSHIPS	**GROUP WINNERS**	**SCORE**		**OPPONENT**
1989-10-06 St. John's, NL	Scarborough Azzurri SC	D 2-2	D	Edm. Ital Canadians SC
1989-10-07 St. John's, NL	Scarborough Azzurri SC	W 4-2	L	Vancouver Westside FC
CHALLENGE TROPHY FINAL	**CHAMPIONS**	**SCORE**		**RUNNERS UP**
1989-10-09 St. John's, NL	Scarborough Azzurri SC	W 3-2	L	Holy Cross FC

Scarborough's goals were scored by Dino Mastrogiaosis, Bart Cramarossa and George Argyropoulos. Most Valuable Player of the National Championships : goalkeeper Greg Tassino.

CANADIAN SOCCER HISTORY
MEN'S AMATEUR FOOTBALL CHAMPIONS

1990s

■ CHALLENGE TROPHY

1990 Vancouver Firefighters
FOURTH NATIONAL CHAMPIONSHIP

MONDAY 8 OCTOBER 1990 - BEAZLEY FIELD IN DARTMOUTH
Rosenlund scored winner in extra time

Vancouver Firefighters FC won their fourth National Championships after they beat hosts Dartmouth United in extra time in the 1990 Canadian Final. Bobby Rosenlund was the hero after he scored the match winner in the 110th minute at Beazley Field. Goalkeeper Randy Keen posted the clean sheet.

Firefighters FC reached the 1990 Canadian Final after they won their group with back-to-back victories over Saint John Bicentennial and Windsor Caboto. Mike Zacharuk was the goalscoring hero in the 1-0 win over Windsor.

Before winning the National Championships, Vancouver Firefighters FC won the 1990 BC Province Cup with a 1-0 win over New Westminster QPR. Zacharuk was the goalscorer. Vancouver won the Western playoff with a 2-1 victory over Edmonton Ital Canadians SC on goals by Colin Elmes and Mike Smith.

CHAMPIONS : VANCOUVER FIREFIGHTERS FC
1990 Vancouver Firefighters FC (unknown lineup for the Final) : GK Randy Keen; Greg Andrews, Ray Brown, Colin Elmes, Mark Etheridge, Marty Etheridge, Steve Fagan, Brent Gant, Bruce Gant, John Kveton, Andy Meyer, Mike Primerano, Gord Quilty captain, Bobby Rosenlund, Dave Rosenlund, Mike Smith, Neil VanDuyhoven, John Zacharuk, Mike Zacharuk. Head Coach Jamie Buchanan, Team Manager Bill Sinclair.

BC PROVINCE CUP FINAL	PROVINCIAL WINNERS	SCORE	RUNNERS UP
1990-05-27 N. Vancouver, BC	Vancouver Firefighters FC	W 1-0 L	New Westminster QPR
INTERPROVINCIAL PLAYDOWNS	**PLAYOFF WINNERS**	**SCORE**	**OPPONENT**
1990-09-15 Edmonton, AB	Vancouver Firefighters FC	W 6-1 L	Saskatoon United SC
1990-09-16 Edmonton, AB	Vancouver Firefighters FC	W 2-1 L	Edm. Ital Canadians SC
CS NATIONAL CHAMPIONSHIPS	**GROUP WINNERS**	**SCORE**	**OPPONENT**
1990-10-06 Dartmouth, NS	Vancouver Firefighters FC	W 5-1 L	Saint John Bicentennial
1990-10-07 Dartmouth, NS	Vancouver Firefighters FC	W 1-0 L	Windsor Caboto Sting
CHALLENGE TROPHY FINAL	**HOME TEAM**	**SCORE**	**AWAY TEAM**
1990-10-08 Dartmouth, NS	Vancouver Firefighters FC	W 1-0 L	Dartmouth United

Vancouver's lone goal in the Final was scored in extra time by Bobby Rosenlund.

NorVan ANAF #45
FIRST NATIONAL CHAMPIONSHIP

MONDAY 14 OCTOBER 1991 - UMEA FIELD IN SASKATOON
NorVan won shootout to capture first title

North Vancouver's Army, Navy & Air Force #45 won their first of back-to-back Canadian titles when they beat former champions Scarborough Azzurri SC in a shootout. The two sides scored two goals each before NorVan ANAF #45 won 4-2 on kicks from the penalty mark in the 1991 Canadian Final.

NorVan goalkeeper Stacy Gowanlock made two saves in the shootout, incidentally the first-ever Challenge Trophy final decided on kicks from the penalty mark. Before the match went into extra time, Peter Clarkman and Clark Brolly scored for the winners.

NorVan ANAF #45 reached the 1991 Canadian Final after they posted back-to-back wins in the group phase. They won 5-1 over Saskatoon Thistle FC and then 5-0 over former champions Winnipeg Lucania SC.

Before winning the 1991 National Championships, NorVan ANAF #45 beat the defending national champions Vancouver Firefighters FC in a shootout in the BC Province Cup Final. Gowanlock made one save in the shootout.

CHAMPIONS : NORVAN ANAF #45
1991 North Vancouver Norvan ANAF #45 (unknown lineup for the Final) : GK Stacy Gowanlock; Nerville Abreo, Dave Ball, Martin Best, Clark Brolly, Eddie Cannon, Peter Clarkman, Barry Deardon, Gordon Deas, Mike Dodd, Mike Geary, Greg Haywood, Scott Macey, Steve Millar, Graeme Slee, Eamonn Ward, Peter Wortman. Head Coach Ian Farquhar. Team Manager Bill McGarva.

BC PROVINCE CUP FINAL	PROVINCIAL WINNERS	SCORE		OPPONENT
1991-05-26 North Vancouver, BC	NorVan ANAF	D	0-0 D	Vancouver Firefighters
NorVan ANAF #45 won 3-1 on kicks from the penalty mark.				
CS NATIONAL CHAMPIONSHIPS	**FIRST STAGE**	**SCORE**		**OPPONENT**
1991-10-11 Saskatoon, SK	NorVan ANAF	W	5-1 L	Saskatoon Thistle FC
CS NATIONAL CHAMPIONSHIPS	**SEMIFINALS**	**SCORE**		**OPPONENT**
1991-10-12 Saskatoon, SK	NorVan ANAF	W	5-0 L	Winnipeg Lucania SC
CHALLENGE TROPHY FINAL	**CHAMPIONS**	**SCORE**		**RUNNERS UP**
1991-10-14 Saskatoon, SK	NorVan ANAF	D	2-2 D	Scarborough Azzurri

North Vancouver's goals in the Final were scored by Peter Clarkman and Clark Brolly. After the 2-2 draw, North Vancouver won 4-2 on kicks from the penalty mark to capture the Challenge Trophy.

1992  NorVan ANAF #45
SECOND NATIONAL CHAMPIONSHIP

MONDAY 12 OCTOBER 1992 - SWANGARD STADIUM IN BURNABY

Millar scored title winner in extra time

Steve Millar was the hero in extra time as NorVan ANAF #45 captured their second-straight Challenge Trophy at Canada Soccer's National Championships. Just one year after winning the title on the road in Saskatoon, North Vancouver won the 1992 Canadian Final closer to home at Swangard Stadium in Burnaby.

For Millar, it was his second-straight title-winning goal at Swangard Stadium in the month of October. Just nine days earlier with professional side Winnipeg Fury SC, Millar scored the goal that beat the Vancouver 86ers for the 1992 Canadian Soccer League championship.

Before winning the National Championships, NorVan ANAF #45 won the 1992 BC Province Cup after they beat Simon Fraser Clan Alumni at Kinsmen Stadium in North Vancouver in late May. Andy Hird scored the 1-0 winner, goalkeeper Don Penner posted the clean sheet, and centre back Mike Geary was named Player of the Match.

More than four months later at Burnaby, NorVan ANAF #45 reached the Canadian Final after they posted back-to-back wins in the group phase over Holy Cross FC and Halifax King of Donair.

CHAMPIONS : NORVAN ANAF #45

1992 North Vancouver Norvan ANAF #45 (unknown lineup for the Final) : 1 GK Dan Penner, 1 GK Didar Sandhu; 2 Gordon Deas, 3 Mike Geary, 4 Greg Haywood, 5 Graeme Slee, 6 Eamonn Ward, 7 Dave Ball, 8 Steve Millar, 9 Clark Brolly, 10 Martin Best, 11 Barry Deardon, 12 Eddie Cannon, 13 Oliver Heald, 17 Simon Tate. Missed Final: 14 Andy Hird, 15 Mike Dodd (injured), 16 Scott Macey (injured). Head Coach Tom Millar, Assistant Pat Morton.

BC PROVINCE CUP FINAL	PROVINCIAL WINNERS	SCORE	RUNNERS UP
1992-05-24 North Vancouver, BC	NorVan ANAF W	1-0 L	Simon Fraser Alumni
CS NATIONAL CHAMPIONSHIPS	**FIRST STAGE**	**SCORE**	**OPPONENT**
1992-10-09 Burnaby, BC	NorVan ANAF W	3-1 L	Holy Cross FC
CS NATIONAL CHAMPIONSHIPS	**SEMIFINALS**	**SCORE**	**OPPONENT**
1992-10-10 Burnaby, BC	NorVan ANAF W	2-1 L	Halifax King of Donair
CHALLENGE TROPHY FINAL	**CHAMPIONS**	**SCORE**	**RUNNERS UP**
1992-10-12 Burnaby, BC	NorVan ANAF W	1-0 L	Edmonton Scottish

North Vancouver's lone goal in the Final was scored in extra time by Steve Millar.

Vancouver Westside FC  1993
FIRST NATIONAL CHAMPIONSHIP

MONDAY 11 OCTOBER 1993 - CENTENNIAL STADIUM IN ETOBICOKE
Johnston scored Westside match winner

Vancouver Westside FC captured Canada Soccer's 1993 National Championships after they beat Longueuil Calommiers on a single goal in the Canadian Final. Bill Johnston scored the winning goal in the 23rd minute and Lee Atterton later hit the crossbar twice as the Vancouver side won 1-0 at Centennial Stadium in Etobicoke.

Forward Alex Percy, who got the assist on the Johnston winner, was named the Most Valuable Player of the National Championships. He led Vancouver with three goals in the group phase.

Vancouver won 5-0 over Saskatoon Hollandia, drew 1-1 with Woodbridge Sora Lazio, and won 6-3 over Halifax King of Donair.

Before winning the National Championships, Vancouver Westside FC captured the 1993 BC Province Cup after they beat two-time Canadian champions NorVan ANAF #45. Johnston scored the 1-1 equaliser in extra time before Westside FC won 4-2 on kicks from the penalty mark.

CHAMPIONS : VANCOUVER WESTSIDE FC
1993 Vancouver Westside FC (unknown lineup for the Final) : 1 GK Mike Wicken; 2 Mike Schrack, 3 Dave Jones, 4 Dan Tuan, 5 Dave Partridge, 6 Colin Pettingale, 7 Mike Araszewski, 8 Mike Mosher, 9 Gary Kern, 10 Doug Schultz, 11 Carl Atterton, 13 Alex Percy, 14 Steve Nesin, 15 Lee Atterton, 17 Bill Johnston, 20 D'Arcy Boulton, 22 Geoff Catliff.

BC PROVINCE CUP FINAL	PROVINCIAL WINNERS	SCORE	RUNNERS UP
1993-05-16 North Vancouver, BC	Vancouver Westside FC D	1-1	D NorVan ANAF
Vancouver won 4-2 on kicks from the penalty mark.			
CS NATIONAL CHAMPIONSHIPS	**GROUP WINNERS**	**SCORE**	**OPPONENT**
1993-10-08 Etobicoke, ON	Vancouver Westside FC W	5-0	L Saskatoon Hollandia
1993-10-09 Etobicoke, ON	Vancouver Westside FC D	1-1	D Woodbridge Sora Lazio
1993-10-10 Etobicoke, ON	Vancouver Westside FC W	6-3	L Halifax King of Donair
CHALLENGE TROPHY FINAL	**CHAMPIONS**	**SCORE**	**RUNNERS UP**
1993-10-11 Etobicoke, ON	Vancouver Westside FC W	1-0	L Calommiers Longueuil

Vancouver Westside FC's lone goal in the Final was scored by Bill Johnston.
Most Valuable Player of the National Championships : Alex Percy.

■ CHALLENGE TROPHY

1994 Edmonton Ital Canadians
FIRST NATIONAL CHAMPIONSHIP

MONDAY 10 OCTOBER 1994 - VICTORIA SOCCER CLUB IN EDMONTON

Falcone scored Edmonton match winner

Edmonton Ital Canadians SC won Canada Soccer's 1994 National Championships in their home city after they beat former champions Scarborough Azzurri SC in the Canadian Final. Daniel Falcone scored the 1-0 match winner in the 28th minute while Wayne Gordey posted the clean sheet at Victoria Soccer Club in Edmonton.

Edmonton Ital Canadians SC were perfect with four wins, four clean sheets, and 10 goals scored at the National Championships. Eight different Edmonton players scored goals at the 1994 tournament. They beat three former champions in Winnipeg Lucania SC, Holy Cross FC and Scarborough Azzurri SC.

Before winning the 1994 National Championships, Edmonton Ital Canadians SC won the six-team Alberta Cup in Calgary during Labour Day weekend. It was Edmonton's second provincial title in a row and their fifth Alberta Cup in seven years since 1988, the year they finished as national runners up behind Holy Cross FC.

CHAMPIONS : EDMONTON ITAL CANADIANS SC

1994 Edmonton Ital Canadians SC (unknown lineup for the Final) : GK Wayne Gordey, GK Bernie Soto; 2 Rocky DeLuca, 5 Eric Munoz, 6 Scott McGeoch, 7 Angelo Sestito, 8 Sergio Maione, 9 Nandor Takats, 10 Andy Takats captain, 11 Norm Odinga, 12 Rob Montalto, 13 Franco Saporito, 14 Joe Parrottino, 15 Daniel Falcone, 16 Robert Biro, 17 Murray David, 19 Vince Reda, 20 Simon Massimino. Did not feature in Final: 0 GK Pat Onstad. Head Coach: Mike Traficante, Assistant Lorenzo Antonello, Team Manager Mimmo Longo, Trainer Mike Bruni.

ALBERTA CUP FINAL	PROVINCIAL WINNERS	SCORE	RUNNERS UP
1994-09-05 Calgary, AB	Edmonton Ital Canadians SC W	? L	Edmonton Scottish SC
CS NATIONAL CHAMPIONSHIPS	**GROUP WINNERS**	**SCORE**	**OPPONENT**
1994-10-07 Edmonton, AB	Edmonton Ital Canadians SC W	1-0 L	Winnipeg Lucania SC
1994-10-08 Edmonton, AB	Edmonton Ital Canadians SC W	4-0 L	Holy Cross FC
1994-10-09 Edmonton, AB	Edmonton Ital Canadians SC W	4-0 L	Mistral Estrie
CHALLENGE TROPHY FINAL	**CHAMPIONS**	**SCORE**	**RUNNERS UP**
1994-10-10 Edmonton, AB	Edmonton Ital Canadians SC W	1-0 L	Scarborough Azzurri

Edmonton's lone goal in the Final was scored by Daniel Falcone.

Mistral Estrie
FIRST NATIONAL CHAMPIONSHIP

MONDAY 9 OCTOBER 1995 - WINNIPEG SPORTS COMPLEX

Messier scored title winner in extra time

Québec's Mistral Estrie captured Canada Soccer's 1995 National Championships after they beat Halifax King of Donair by a single goal in extra time. Alain Messier was the hero after he scored the match winner in the 100th minute at the Winnipeg Sports Complex in Manitoba.

Mistral Estrie were the first Québec team to capture Canada Soccer's Challenge Trophy in 34 years since professional side Montréal Concordia FC won the 1961 Canadian Final.

Mistral Estrie reached the 1995 Canadian Final after they won their group with two wins and just one loss. Eric Puig scored a hat trick in the 3-1 win over the St. Lawrence Laurentians while Amédée Nyamat scored a hat trick in the 7-1 win over Winnipeg Polonia. Nyamat also scored in the 4-1 loss to Edmonton Ital Canadians SC, the defending national champions.

Before winning the 1995 National Championships, Mistral Estrie finished in first place in the LSEQ (Ligue de soccer élite du Québec) ahead of runners up CS Hermès Montréal. In the provincial championship, they won 4-2 over Racing de Montréal.

CHAMPIONS : MISTRAL ESTRIE

1995 Mistral Estrie (unknown lineup for the Final) · 1 GK Richard Audit, 1 GK Robert Holtman; 2 Alain Desbois, 4 René Dugrennier, 5 Stéphane Fortier, 6 André Sylvain, 7 Lionel Hugonnier, 8 Steve Pouliot, 9 Johnny Tasovlis, 10 Richard Pierre-Gilles, 11 Luc Chabot, 12 Julien Rheault, 13 Daniel Corture, 14 Steve Dubuc, 15 Eric Puig, 16 Alain Messier, 18 Mathieu Hade, 20 Amédée Nyamat. Head Coach Guy Smith, Assistant Jacques Duquette, Trainer Grant Robinson.

COUPE DU QUÉBEC	PROVINCIAL WINNERS	SCORE	OPPONENT
1995-09-10 Laval, QC	Mistral Estrie W	4-2	L Racing de Montréal
CS NATIONAL CHAMPIONSHIPS	**GROUP WINNERS**	**SCORE**	**OPPONENT**
1995-10-06 Winnipeg, MB	Mistral Estrie W	3-1	L St. Lawrence Laurentiens
1995-10-07 Winnipeg, MB	Mistral Estrie W	7-2	L Winnipeg Polonia
1995-10-08 Winnipeg, MB	Mistral Estrie L	1-4	W Edm. Ital Canadians SC
CHALLENGE TROPHY FINAL	**CHAMPIONS**	**SCORE**	**RUNNERS UP**
1995-10-09 Winnipeg, MB	Mistral Estrie W	1-0	L Halifax King of Donair

Mistral Estrie's lone goal in the Final was scored in extra time by Alain Messier.

■ CHALLENGE TROPHY

1996 Vancouver Westside FC
SECOND NATIONAL CHAMPIONSHIP

MONDAY 14 OCTOBER 1996 - LOCKHART RYAN MEMORIAL PARK
Westside won second title on Catliff brace

Vancouver Westside FC won their second Challenge Trophy in four years after they beat Cosmos LaSalle at Canada Soccer's 1996 National Championships. Concacaf champion John Catliff was the hero after he scored both Westside goals in the 2-1 victory at Lockhart Ryan Memorial Park in in New Minas, Nova Scotia.

Catliff was also named the Most Valuable Player of the National Championships after he finished the tournament with six goals: two against Scarborough, two against Halifax, and two against LaSalle in the Canadian Final. Vancouver won 3-1 over Scarborough Azzurri, won 5-1 over the St. Lawrence Laurentians, and drew 3-3 with Halifax King of Donair.

Before winning the National Championships, Vancouver Westside FC captured the BC Province Cup provincial championship after they won 2-0 over North Shore Pegasus. Mike Mosher and Steve Kindel were the goalscorers.

CHAMPIONS : VANCOUVER WESTSIDE FC
1996 Vancouver Westside FC (unknown lineup for the Final) : 1 GK Mike Wicken; 2 James Prescott, 4 Steve Dewar, 4 Markus Felderer, 5 Colin Elmes, 6 Joel Hughes, 7 Gary Kern, 8 Mike Mosher, 10 Doug Schultz, 11 Colin Pettingale, 12 Rob Hall, 13 Alex Percy, 14 Tom Pinkerton, 15 Steve Kindel, 16 Tom Kim, 17 Bill Johnston, 18 John Catliff, 22 Geoff Catliff. Head Coach Doug Johnston, Manager Don Johnston.

BC PROVINCE CUP FINAL	PROVINCIAL WINNERS	SCORE	RUNNERS UP
1996-05-12 Coquitlam, BC	Vancouver Westside FC	W 2-0	L North Shore Pegasus
CS NATIONAL CHAMPIONSHIPS	**GROUP WINNERS**	**SCORE**	**OPPONENT**
1996-10-11 New Minas, NS	Vancouver Westside FC	W 3-1	L Scarborough Azzurri
1996-10-12 New Minas, NS	Vancouver Westside FC	W 5-1	L St. Lawrence Laurentiens
1996-10-13 New Minas, NS	Vancouver Westside FC	D 3-3	D Halifax King of Donair
CHALLENGE TROPHY FINAL	**CHAMPIONS**	**SCORE**	**RUNNERS UP**
1996-10-14 New Minas, NS	Vancouver Westside FC	W 2-1	L Cosmos LaSalle

Vancouver's two goals in the Final were scored by John Catliff.
Most Valuable Player of the National Championships : John Catliff.

Edmonton Ital Canadians
SECOND NATIONAL CHAMPIONSHIP  1997

MONDAY 13 OCTOBER 1997 - CALGARY SOCCER CENTRE
Edmonton captured their second title

Edmonton Ital Canadians SC won their second Challenge Trophy in four years after they beat North Shore Pegasus in Canada Soccer's 1997 National Championships at Calgary. Edmonton won 3-1 in the Canadian Final with goals scored by Vince Reda, Norm Odinga and Sergio Maione. Teen goalkeeper Lars Hirschfeld was beaten only once by Surrey's Troy Wood.

Edmonton reached the Canadian Final after they won their group with a draw and two wins. They opened the tournament with a 1-1 draw against former champions Winnipeg Lucania SC, then won 3-1 over CS Rivière-des-Prairies and 1-0 over Hamilton Dundas United.

Before winning the 1997 National Championships, Edmonton Ital Canadians SC won the six-team Alberta Cup provincial championship in Calgary during Labour Day weekend. It was Edmonton's fourth Alberta title in the past five years and their 10th title in 14 years since 1984.

CHAMPIONS : EDMONTON ITAL CANADIANS SC
1997 Edmonton Ital Canadians SC (unknown lineup for the Final) : 1 GK Lars Hirschfeld; 5 Murray David, 7 Angelo Sestito, 8 Sergio Maione, 9 Nandor Takats, 10 Andy Takats, 11 Norm Odinga, 12 Nick Culo, 13 Franco Saporito, 14 Joe Parrottino, 15 Rob Giordano, 16 Marco Quintella, 17 Salvi Cammerata, 18 Dino Maione, 19 Vince Reda, 20 Mateo Saccomano, 21 Simon Massimino, Did not feature in Final: 0 GK Bernie Soto. Head Coach Mike Traficante, Assistant Mimmo Longo, Team Manager Ignazio Marino.

ALBERTA CUP FINAL	PROVINCIAL WINNERS	SCORE		
1997-09-01 Calgary, AB	Edmonton Ital Canadians SC	finish in first place		
CS NATIONAL CHAMPIONSHIPS	**GROUP WINNERS**		**SCORE**	**OPPONENT**
1997-10-09 Calgary, AB	Edmonton Ital Canadians SC	D	1-1 D	Winnipeg Lucania SC
1997-10-10 Calgary, AB	Edmonton Ital Canadians SC	W	3-1 L	CS Rivière-des-Prairies
1997-10-11 Calgary, AB	Edmonton Ital Canadians SC	W	1-0 L	Hamilton Dundas United
CHALLENGE TROPHY FINAL	**CHAMPIONS**		**SCORE**	**RUNNERS UP**
1997-10-13 Calgary, AB	Edmonton Ital Canadians SC	W	3-1 L	North Shore Pegasus

Edmonton's goals in the Final were scored by Vince Reda, Norm Odinga and Sergio Maione.

■ **CHALLENGE TROPHY**

1998 *CS Rivière-des-Prairies*
FIRST NATIONAL CHAMPIONSHIP

MONDAY 12 OCTOBER 1998 - CHAPMAN FIELD IN FREDERICTON
Villalba scored RDP match winner

Montréal's CS Rivière-des-Prairies won Canada Soccer's 1998 National Championships after they beat Hamilton Serbian by a single goal in the Canadian Final. Player of the Match Wilfredo Villalba was the hero after he scored the 1-0 match winner in Fredericton. Sergio Grande, in goal for the injured Remy Eyckerman, posted the clean sheet.

Gustavo Echevarría was the tournament's top scorer with six goals from the group phase. He scored once in a 2-2 draw with Vancouver Firefighters FC, four times in a 7-3 win over Saskatoon Arauco, and once more in a 2-0 win over St. Lawrence Laurentians. Both Rivière-des-Prairies and Vancouver finished the group phase tied on points, but RDP advanced to the Canadian Final with a better goals difference.

Before winning the National Championships, CS Rivière-des-Prairies won the 1998 Québec Cup provincial championship after they finished at the top of a four-team, round-robin series in Rock Forest. Following the decisive match with both CS Rivière-des-Prairies and Corfinium St-Léonard tied on points, RDP won 4-3 on kicks as Eyckerman made two saves in the shootout.

CHAMPIONS : CS RIVIÈRE-DES-PRAIRIES
1998 Rivière-des-Prairies (unknown lineup for the Final) : 12 GK Sergio Grande, 18 GK Rémy Eckerman; 2 Luigi Spinelli, 3 Rachid Lahbabi, 4 Jean-Robert Merisier, 5 Gino Nue, 6 Guillermo Nue, 7 Manuel Gonzalez, 8 Bruno Nue, 9 Yacine Hamrouni, 10 Carlos Nue, 11 Sandro Ferrante, 12 Wilfredo Villalba, 14 Alix Azor, 15 Gustavo Echevarria, 16 Fernando Dominiari, 19 Jadverne Lafortune. Head Coach Paolo Ferrante, Team Manager Sabino Grassi.

COUPE DU QUÉBEC	PROVINCIAL WINNERS			
1998-09-13 Rock Forest, QC	CS Rivière-des-Prairies	finish in first place		
CS NATIONAL CHAMPIONSHIPS	**GROUP WINNERS**		**SCORE**	**OPPONENT**
1998-10-09 Fredericton, NB	CS Rivière-des-Prairies	D	2-2 D	Vancouver Firefighters
1998-10-10 Fredericton, NB	CS Rivière-des-Prairies	W	7-3 L	Saskatoon Arauco
1998-10-11 Fredericton, NB	CS Rivière-des-Prairies	W	2-0 L	St. Lawrence Laurentians
CHALLENGE TROPHY FINAL	**CHAMPIONS**		**SCORE**	**RUNNERS UP**
1998-10-12 Fredericton, NB	CS Rivière-des-Prairies	W	1-0 L	Hamilton Serbian

Rivière-des-Prairies' lone goal in the Final was scored by Wilfredo Villalba.

Calgary Celtic SFC
FIRST NATIONAL CHAMPIONSHIP

MONDAY 11 OCTOBER 1999 - TOWNSEND PARK IN CHILLIWACK

Patik scored match winner for Calgary

Calgary Celtic SFC won Canada Soccer's 1999 National Championships after they beat Coquitlam Metro-Ford SC on a single goal in the Canadian Final. Cenek Patik was the hero as Celtic became the first Calgary-based team in 25 years to win the Challenge Trophy.

Doug Auvigne was later named the Most Valuable Player of the 1999 National Championships in Chilliwack. Mark Slade and Gareth Sloan were the team leaders with three goals each. Calgary reached the Canadian Final after they won their group with four-straight wins against Halifax Dunbrack, Moncton Rovers, Woodbridge Sora Lazio, and Winnipeg Lucania SC.

Before winning the National Championships, Calgary Celtic SFC won the six-team Alberta Cup provincial championship in Calgary during Labour Day weekend. They were back-to-back Alberta Major Soccer League champions after they finished first overall in the league standings in both 1998 and 1999.

CHAMPIONS : CALGARY CELTIC SFC (CALLIES)
1999 Calgary Celtic SFC (unknown lineup for the Final) : 0 GK Dave Harrison; 2 Glen Hawkins, 4 Cenek Patik, 6 John Oliverio, 7 Doug Auvigne, 9 Mark Slade, 10 Steffen Holdt, 11 Gareth Sloan, 12 Liam de Silva, 13 Felix Gelt, 15 Mike Rodway, 16 Chris Rodway, 18 Mike Howlett, 19 Noel Crisdale, 20 Ziggy Funk, 21 Felix Napuri. Did not feature in Final. 0 GK Doug Bourne. Head Coach Dave Randall, Assistant Dave Morrow, Team Manager Gord Rodway, Trainer Steve Oakey.

ALBERTA CUP FINAL	HOME TEAM	SCORE	AWAY TEAM
1999-09-06 Calgary, AB	Calgary Celtic SFC	W 3-2 L	Calgary Dinosaurs
CS NATIONAL CHAMPIONSHIPS	**GROUP WINNERS**	**SCORE**	**OPPONENT**
1999-10-06 Chilliwack, BC	Calgary Celtic SFC	W 1-0 L	Halifax Dunbrack SC
1999-10-07 Chilliwack, BC	Calgary Celtic SFC	W 4-1 L	Moncton Rovers
1999-10-08 Chilliwack, BC	Calgary Celtic SFC	W 3-1 L	Woodbridge Sora Lazio
1999-10-10 Chilliwack, BC	Calgary Celtic SFC	W 5-1 L	Winnipeg Lucania SC
CHALLENGE TROPHY FINAL	**CHAMPIONS**	**SCORE**	**RUNNERS UP**
1999-10-11 Chilliwack, BC	Calgary Celtic SFC	W 1-0 L	Coquitlam Metro-Ford SC

Calgary's lone goal in the Final was scored by Cenek Patik.
Most Valuable Player of the Men's National Championships : Doug Auvigne.

CANADIAN SOCCER HISTORY
MEN'S AMATEUR FOOTBALL CHAMPIONS

2000s

■ CHALLENGE TROPHY

2000 *Winnipeg Lucania SC*
SECOND NATIONAL CHAMPIONSHIP

MONDAY 9 OCTOBER 2000 - UMEA EAST PARK IN SASKATOON
Winnipeg Lucania won their second title
• •

Winnipeg Lucania SC won their second Challenge Trophy in 14 years after they beat two-time winners Vancouver Westside FC at Canada Soccer's 2000 National Championships. Damien Rocke and Hadyn Sloane-Searle were the goalscorers in the 2-0 victory at Saskatoon.

At the National Championships, Winnipeg lost their opening match to Halifax King of Donair, then won three-straight group matches against PEI's Eastern Eagles, defending champions Calgary Celtic SFC, and hosts Saskatoon Arsenal. Winnipeg qualified for the Canadian Final with their win over Saskatoon, but they lost captain Marcello Paolucci to a suspension after he picked up his third yellow card in four matches.

Before winning the 2000 National Championships, Winnipeg Lucania SC captured the two-leg Manitoba Cup provincial championship after they won 2-0 on aggregate over Winnipeg Sons of Italy. It was their seventh provincial title in 14 years.

CHAMPIONS : WINNIPEG LUCANIA SC
2000 Winnipeg Lucania SC (unknown lineup for the Final) : 00 GK Brian Oleksiuk, 1 GK Jeff Seney, 18 GK Hadyn Sloane-Seale, 3 Ethan Rocke, 4 Dominic Allen, 5 Mike Kovac, 6 Bill Klymcuk, 7 Serge Bohemier, 8 Joel Bohemier, 9 Jordan Goetting, 10 Marcello Paolucci captain, 11 John Berti, 12 Russell Harder, 14 Nick Scott, 15 Emilio Patella, 16 Jamie DeSilva, 17 Desmond Clarke, 19 Damian Rocke. Head Coach Kevin MacKay, Team Manager Michael Nardiello, Trainer Jen Turcotte.

MANITOBA CUP FINAL	PROVINCIAL WINNERS	SCORE		OPPONENT
2000-08-25 Winnipeg, MB	Winnipeg Lucania SC	2-0		Winnipeg Sons of Italy
2000-08-27 Winnipeg, MB	Winnipeg Lucania SC	0-0		Winnipeg Sons of Italy

Winnipeg Lucania SC won 2-0 on aggregate.

CS NATIONAL CHAMPIONSHIPS	GROUP WINNERS	SCORE		OPPONENT
2000-10-04 Saskatoon, SK	Winnipeg Lucania SC	L 0-1	W	Halifax King of Donair
2000-10-06 Saskatoon, SK	Winnipeg Lucania SC	W 3-0	L	Eastern Eagles
2000-10-07 Saskatoon, SK	Winnipeg Lucania SC	W 2-1	L	Calgary Celtic SFC
2000-10-08 Saskatoon, SK	Winnipeg Lucania SC	W 2-1	L	Saskatoon Arsenal

CHALLENGE TROPHY FINAL	CHAMPIONS	SCORE		RUNNERS UP
2000-10-09 Saskatoon, SK	Winnipeg Lucania SC	W 2-0	L	Vancouver Westside FC

Winnipeg's goals in the Final were scored by Damien Rocke and Hadyn Sloane Searle.

CHALLENGE TROPHY

Halifax King of Donair
FIRST NATIONAL CHAMPIONSHIP  2001

MONDAY 8 OCTOBER 2001 - VAUGHAN GROVE IN VAUGHAN
Halifax won Nova Scotia their first title

Halifax King of Donair became the first Nova Scotia club to win Canada Soccer's National Championships when they beat Victoria Gorge FC in the 2001 Canadian Final. Trevor Reddick (two), Mike Hasiuk and Mesut Mert were the goalscorers in the 4-1 victory just north of Toronto.

Halifax, Edmonton Victoria SC and defending champions Winnipeg Lucania SC all finished tied on points, but Halifax won the group based on goals difference. Halifax pulled away on the final day with a 5-1 win over Saskatoon Arsenal on goals by Hasiuk (two) and Colin March (three).

Before winning the 2001 National Championships, Halifax King of Donair captured the two-leg Nova Scotia Challenge Cup after they won 4-2 on aggregate over Halifax Dunbrack. It was King of Donair's 10th provincial title in 19 years.

CHAMPIONS : HALIFAX KING OF DONAIR
2001 Halifax King of Donair (unknown lineup for the Final) : 00 GK Mark Gardiner, 2 Ewan Lyttle, 3 Tim Stephenson, 4 Mike Hasiuk captain, 5 Tim Mullen, 6 Trevor Reddick, 7 Ian Clark, 8 Jay Robinson, 10 Idris Mert, 11 Rob Adams, 12 Blake Geddis, 13 Mesut Mert, 14 Colin March, 15 Eduardo Farias, 16 Dzevad Imocanin, 19 Danny Fournier, 20 Peter Lawrence, 00 GK Glen Sullivan; . Did not feature in Final: 9 Gray Zurheide, 17 Michael Brabant. Head Coach Tony Eghan, Assistant George Iatrou, Team Manager Mourad Fario, President Angelo Cianfaglione. Did not attend: Carl MacGillvrray, Brian Wishart.

NOVA SCOTIA CUP FINAL	PROVINCIAL WINNERS	SCORE	RUNNERS UP
2001-08-31 Halifax, NS	Halifax King of Donair	2-2	Halifax Dunbrack SC
2001-09-02 Halifax, NS	Halifax King of Donair	2-0	Halifax Dunbrack SC

Halifax King of Donair won 4-2 on aggregate.

CS NATIONAL CHAMPIONSHIPS	GROUP WINNERS	SCORE	OPPONENT
2001-10-03 Vaughan, ON	Halifax King of Donair	D 2-2	D Edmonton Victoria SC
2001-10-05 Vaughan, ON	Halifax King of Donair	W 1-0	L Eastern Eagles
2001-10-06 Vaughan, ON	Halifax King of Donair	D 0-0	D Winnipeg Lucania SC
2001-10-07 Vaughan, ON	Halifax King of Donair	W 5-1	L Saskatoon Arsenal

CHALLENGE TROPHY FINAL	CHAMPIONS	SCORE	RUNNERS UP
2001-10-08 Vaughan, ON	Halifax King of Donair	W 4-1	L Victoria Gorge FC

Halifax's goals in the Final were scored by Trevor Reddick (two), Mike Hasiuk and Mesut Mert.

— CHALLENGE TROPHY

2002  Winnipeg Sons of Italy
FIRST NATIONAL CHAMPIONSHIP

MONDAY 14 OCTOBER 2002 - KING GEORGE V PARK IN ST. JOHN'S

Margison scored golden goal winner

Sean Margison was the golden goal hero when the Winnipeg Sons of Italy captured Canada Soccer's 2002 National Championships in front of a packed crowd at King George V Park. Margison scored the winning goal while captain Steve Sawatzky posted the clean sheet for the 1-0 victory over the St. Lawrence Laurentians.

With roughly 7,000 spectators in attendance, it was believed to be the largest crowd for the Challenge Trophy Final in 55 years. Most of the Newfoundland crowd were in town to support the Laurentians, who previously lost the Canadian Final in 1975 and 1977.

Margison was also the goalscoring hero in the Semifinals when Winnipeg beat the 2001 champions Halifax King of Donair. He scored both goals in that 2-1 victory.

Before winning the 2002 National Championships, Winnipeg Sons of Italy beat the two-time national champions Winnipeg Lucania SC in the Manitoba Cup provincial championship.

CHAMPIONS : WINNIPEG SONS OF ITALY

2002 Winnipeg Sons of Italy (unknown lineup for the Final) : 1 GK Steve Sawatzky; 2 Tevin Olivier-Job, 3 Andrew Aitken, 4 Peter Drazic, 5 Tony Nocita, 6 Jason Colosimo, 7 Edward Keeper, 8 Jordan Lanoway, 9 Robert Cowie, 10 Jorge Aguirre, 11 Justin Parry, 12 Mauricio Aguirre, 14 Steve Rebizant, 16 Ryan Dyck, 17 Sean Margison, 20 Mauricio Martinez, 22 Sean Sylvestre. Head Coach Chic Devenney, Assistant Larry Ladobruk, Team Manager Jozef Kostek, Trainer Chico Colosimo. Missed Final: Ryan Bilous, Emsad Cajic, Mark Zubach.

MANITOBA CUP FINAL	PROVINCIAL WINNERS	SCORE		RUNNERS UP
2002-08-25 Winnipeg, MB	Winnipeg Sons of Italy	W	L	Winnipeg Lucania SC
CS NATIONAL CHAMPIONSHIPS	**GROUP WINNERS**	**SCORE**		**OPPONENT**
2002-10-10 St. John's, NL	Winnipeg Sons of Italy	L 1-0	L	Moncton First Touch
2002-10-11 St. John's, NL	Winnipeg Sons of Italy	D 1-1	D	London Portuguese
CS NATIONAL CHAMPIONSHIPS		**SEMIFINALS**	**SCORE**	**OPPONENT**
2002-10-13 St. John's, NL	Winnipeg Sons of Italy	W 2-1	L	Halifax King of Donair
CHALLENGE TROPHY FINAL		**CHAMPIONS**	**SCORE**	**RUNNERS UP**
2002-10-14 St. John's, NL	Winnipeg Sons of Italy	W 1-0	L	St. Lawrence Laurentiens

Winnipeg's lone goal in the Final was scored in extra time by Sean Margison.

Calgary Caledonian FC  2003
SECOND NATIONAL CHAMPIONSHIP

MONDAY 13 OCTOBER 2003 - PATRO FIELD IN QUÉBEC CITY
Calgary won 4-2 on kicks to capture title

The Calgary Callies won their second Challenge Trophy in five years after they beat Panellinios Montréal FC in a shootout at Canada Soccer's 2003 National Championships. Goalkeeper Dave Harrison was the hero after he made two saves for the 4-2 win on kicks from the penalty mark. It was just the second Final ever decided on kicks from penalty mark.

Harrison was later named the Most Valuable Player of the National Championships. In two shootouts during the group phase, Calgary lost their opener 4-3 to Panellinios (after a 3-3 draw), but then won 4-3 over Halifax Celtic (after a 2-2 draw).

Before winning the National Championships, the Callies won the 2003 Alberta Cup provincial championship in Calgary during Labour Day weekend. It was their fourth provincial title in five years, two of which they won when they were previously known as Calgary Celtic SFC.

CHAMPIONS : CALGARY CALEDONIAN FC (CALLIES)
2003 Calgary Caledonian FC (unknown lineup for the Final) : GK Dave Harrison; 3 Wesley Stephens, 4 Cenek Patik, 5 Noel Grisdale, 7 Jim Reyes, 8 Ben Duffy, 9 Mark Slade, 10 Steffen Holdt, 11 Mike Howlett, 12 Tony Chimera, 13 Jamie Fiddler, 14 Luis Rodriguez, 15 Mike Rodway, 16 Felix Napuri, 17 Justin Cloutier, 20 Chris Kooy. Did not feature in the Final: GK Spencer Arnold. Head Coach Dave Randall, Assistant Dave Morrow, Team Manager Gord Rodway, Trainer Stefan Regnier.

ALBERTA CUP FINAL	PROVINCIAL WINNERS	SCORE	RUNNERS UP
2003-09-01 Calgary, AR	Calgary Caledonian FC	W 1-0 L	Calgary Villains
CS NATIONAL CHAMPIONSHIPS	**GROUP STAGE**	**SCORE**	**TEAM**
2003-10-09 Québec, QC	Calgary Caledonian FC	D 3-3 D	Panellinios Montréal FC
2003-10-10 Québec, QC	Calgary Caledonian FC	D 2-2 D	Halifax Celtic

In the group stage, Calgary lost 4-3 on kicks to Montréal, then won 4-3 on kicks over Halifax. After Halifax protested the tie-breaking scenario, a Calgary-Halifax playoff was scheduled for 11 October.

2003-10-11 Québec, QC	Calgary Caledonian FC	W 1-0 L	Halifax Celtic
CS NATIONAL CHAMPIONSHIPS	**SEMIFINALS**	**SCORE**	**OPPONENT**
2003-10-12 Québec, QC	Calgary Caledonian FC	W 1-0 L	Winnipeg Sokol SC
CHALLENGE TROPHY FINAL	**CHAMPIONS**	**SCORE**	**RUNNERS UP**
2003-10-13 Québec, QC	Calgary Caledonian FC	D 1-1 D	Panellinios Montréal FC

Calgary's goal in the Final was scored by Steffen Holdt. After the 1-1 draw, Calgary Callies FC won 4-2 on kicks to capture the Challenge Trophy.

■ CHALLENGE TROPHY

2004 *Surrey FC Pegasus*
FIRST NATIONAL CHAMPIONSHIP

MONDAY 11 OCTOBER 2004 - UNIVERSITY OF PEI IN CHARLOTTETOWN

Pegasus won 4-3 on kicks to capture title

Surrey FC Pegasus won 4-3 on kicks to capture Canada Soccer's 2004 National Championships after a scoreless draw in the Canadian Final with the Ottawa Royals. Jamie Fiddler scored the 4-3 winner before Ottawa missed on their final attempt.

At the National Championships, Surrey won their four group matches against Halifax Celtic, Fundy United, Panellinios Montréal FC, and Marystown United. Surrey scored 16 goals in those four matches led by Mike Dodd (four goals) and Paul Dailly (three goals).

The 2004 Canadian Final marked the second year in a row that the Challenge Trophy was decided on kicks from the penalty mark.

Before winning the 2004 National Championships, Surrey FC Pegasus captured the BC Province Cup with a 3-0 victory over two-time national champions Vancouver Westside FC.

CHAMPIONS : SURREY FC PEGASUS

2004 Surrey FC Pegasus (unknown lineup for the Final) : 1 GK Steve London, 0 GK Shawn Perry; 3 Trevor Short, 5 Gavin Frey, 6 Eddie Cannon, 7 Paul Dailly, 8 Darin Burr, 9 Adam Costley, 10 Ryan Powell, 12 Nicolas Berg, 13 Mike Dodd, 14 Ryan Green, 15 Robin Regnier, 17 Jamie Fiddler, 18 Stedman Espinoza, 20 Laurent Scalignine, 21 Rob Reed. Did not feature in the Final: 2 Rob Iorio, 16 Frank Lore. Head Coach David Fiorvento, Assistant Peter Costley, Team Manager Carmine Clement, Trainer Brad Baker.

BC PROVINCE CUP FINAL	PROVINCIAL WINNERS	SCORE	RUNNERS UP
2004-05-15 Burnay, BC	Surrey FC Pegasus W	3-0 L	Vancouver Westside FC
CS NATIONAL CHAMPIONSHIPS	**GROUP WINNERS**	**SCORE**	**OPPONENT**
2004-10-06 Montague, PE	Surrey FC Pegasus W	3-2 L	Halifax Celtic
2004-10-07 Montague, PE	Surrey FC Pegasus W	6-1 L	Fundy United
2004-10-08 Stratford, PE	Surrey FC Pegasus W	3-0 L	Panellinios Montréal FC
2004-10-10 Charlottetown, PE	Surrey FC Pegasus W	4-2 L	Marystown United
CHALLENGE TROPHY FINAL	**CHAMPIONS**	**SCORE**	**RUNNERS UP**
2004-10-11 Charlottetown, PE	Surrey FC Pegasus D	0-0 D	Ottawa Royals

Surrey Pegasus won 4-3 on kicks from the penalty mark to capture the Challenge Trophy.

Scarborough GS United
FIRST NATIONAL CHAMPIONSHIP

MONDAY 10 OCTOBER 2005 - BROADVIEW PARK IN CALGARY
Haitham scored winner in extra time

Scarborough GS United captured Canada Soccer's 2005 National Championships in extra time after Sultan Haitham scored the 3-2 match winner at Broadview Park in Calgary. Tom Kouzmanis and Emil Calixerio were the goalscorers in the first half before 10-man Scarborough beat the Edmonton Green & Gold on Haitham's winner.

Kouzmanis, a former National Team player, led Scarborough with three goals in four matches. His brother Gus was one of six Scarborough players who scored two goals in four matches.

Scarborough GS United were the first Ontario team since Scarborough Azzurri SC back in 1989 to win the Challenge Trophy.

Before winning the National Championships, Scarborough GS United captured the 2005 Ontario Cup provincial championship with a 1-0 victory over Woodbridge Azzurri. Tom Kouzmanis was the golden goal hero when he scored the match winner in extra time.

CHAMPIONS : SCARBOROUGH GS UNITED
2005 Scarborough GS United (unknown lineup for the Final) : 1 GK Courtney Campbell, 2 Courtney Brown, 5 Anthony Marshall, 6 Valentine Anozie, 7 Emil Calixerio, 8 Lyndon Hooper, 9 Ryan Dummett, 10 Decio Rego, 11 Tom Kouzmanis, 12 Jonathan Westmass, 14 Sultan Haitham, 15 Shawn Long, 16 Ron Belfon, 17 Jermaine Coleman, 19 Shaun Griffith, 20 Richard Kirwan, 21 Gus Kouzmanis. Head Coach John Williams, Assistant Chris Handsor, Assistant Michael Chivers, Team Manager Beldev Sidhu.

ONTARIO CUP FINAL	PROVINCIAL WINNERS	SCORE	RUNNERS UP
2005-09-17 Vaughan, ON	Scarborough GS United	W 1-0 L	Woodbridge Azzurri
CS NATIONAL CHAMPIONSHIPS	**GROUP WINNERS**	**SCORE**	**OPPONENT**
2005-10-06 Calgary, AB	Scarborough GS United	W 5-0 L	Hampton United
2005-10-08 Calgary, AB	Scarborough GS United	W 4-0 L	Eastern Eagles
CS NATIONAL CHAMPIONSHIPS	**SEMIFINALS**	**SCORE**	**OPPONENT**
2005-10-09 Calgary, AB	Scarborough GS United	W 3-1 L	Panellinios Montréal FC
CHALLENGE TROPHY FINAL	**CHAMPIONS**	**SCORE**	**RUNNERS UP**
2005-10-10 Calgary, AB	Scarborough GS United	W 3-2 L	Edmonton Green & Gold

Scarborough's goals were scored by Emil Calixerio, Tom Kouzmanis and Sultan Haitham.

– CHALLENGE TROPHY

2006 Ottawa St. Anthony SC
FIRST NATIONAL CHAMPIONSHIP

MONDAY 9 OCTOBER 2006 - NEWTON ATHLETIC PARK IN SURREY
Some scored St. Anthony's title winner

Ottawa St. Anthony Italia captured Canada Soccer's 2006 National Championships after they beat two-time winners Calgary Callies by a single goal in the Canadian Final. Captain Urbain Some scored the lone goal while goalkeeper Angus Wong posted the clean sheet in the 1-0 victory at Newton Athletic Park in Surrey.

St. Anthony Italia, who reached the Quarterfinals back in 1964, were the first Ottawa team to win the Challenge Trophy.

On the road to winning the 2006 Challenge Trophy, Ottawa beat former national champions Scarborough GS United (Ontario Cup), Vancouver Firefighters FC (group phase), Winnipeg Lucania SC (group phase), and Calgary Callies FC (Canadian Final).

In the 2006 Ontario Cup Final, Ottawa St. Anthony Italia beat the 2005 national champions Scarborough GS United on a golden goal scored by Johnny Schienda.

CHAMPIONS : OTTAWA ST. ANTHONY ITALIA FC
2006 Ottawa St. Anthony SC (unknown lineup for the Final) : 0 GK Scott Milliquet, 1 GK Angus Wong; 2 Kwesi Loney, 3 Kwame Telemaque, 4 Ladislav Kikunda, 5 Alessandro Bahisti, 6 Simon Bonk, 7 Christian Hoefler, 8 Loui Legakis, 9 Abraham Osman, 10 Johnny Schieda, 11 Souleymane Gagou, 12 Edgar Soglo, 15 Daniel Jones, 17 Richard Furano, 18 Claudio Venegas, 19 Urbain Some, 20 Marcello Plada, 22 Allan Popazzi. Head Coach Aldo Popazzi, Assistant Giovani Schieda, Team Manager Americo Giamberardino, Trainer Arisadi Babitski. Did not travel: Alain Njima, Jeff Sweeney.

ONTARIO CUP FINAL	PROVINCIAL WINNERS	SCORE		RUNNERS UP
2006-09-17 Vaughan, ON	Ottawa St. Anthony SC	W 3-2	L	Scarborough GS United
CS NATIONAL CHAMPIONSHIPS	**GROUP WINNERS**	**SCORE**		**OPPONENT**
2006-10-04 Surrey, BC	Ottawa St. Anthony SC	W 5-3	L	Vancouver Firefighters
2006-10-05 Surrey, BC	Ottawa St. Anthony SC	W 4-0	L	Winnipeg Lucania SC
2006-10-06 Surrey, BC	Ottawa St. Anthony SC	D 0-0	D	Sapperton Rovers
CS NATIONAL CHAMPIONSHIPS	**SEMIFINALS**	**SCORE**		**OPPONENT**
2006-10-08 Surrey, BC	Ottawa St. Anthony SC	W 2-0	L	Scotia M-I Men
CHALLENGE TROPHY FINAL	**CHAMPIONS**	**SCORE**		**RUNNERS UP**
2006-10-09 Surrey, BC	Ottawa St. Anthony SC	W 1-0	L	Calgary Caledonian FC

Ottawa's lone goal in the Final was scored by Urbain Some.

Calgary Caledonian FC
THIRD NATIONAL CHAMPIONSHIP

MONDAY 8 OCTOBER 2007 - MAINLAND COMMONS IN HALIFAX

Slade scored Calgary hat trick in Final

Calgary Caledonian FC won Canada Soccer's National Championships in 2007 when they beat four-time winners Vancouver Columbus FC with five unanswered goals. Mark Slade (three), Cenek Patik and Nicky Reyes were the goalscorers while goalkeeper Dave Harrison posted the clean sheet for the 5-0 victory.

Slade earned Man of the Match honours in the Canadian Final and he was named Most Valuable Player of the National Championships. He was the sixth player in the history of the competition to score a hat trick on the last day of the Canadian Final, albeit the first to do so in 31 years.

Before winning the National Championships, Calgary Callies won the 2007 Alberta Cup provincial championship in Edmonton during Labour Day weekend. The Callies were eight-time Alberta Major Soccer League winners in a 10-year span from 1998 to 2007.

CHAMPIONS : CALGARY CALEDONIAN FC (CALLIES)

2007 Calgary Caledonian FC (unknown lineup for the Final) : 1 GK Dave Harrison, 1 GK Will Langford; 2 Jamie MacDonald, 3 Brett Colvin, 4 Cenek Patik, 5 André Duberry, 7 Nicky Reyes, 8 Jamie Auvigne, 9 Mark Slade, 10 Steffen Holdt, 11 Felix Napuri, 12 Liam De Silva, 13 Francisco Miron, 14 Johnny Cherkas, 15 Stuart Stormonth, 16 Youseff Tarraf, 17 Milan Timotijevic, 18 Eric Roa, 20 Chris Kooy, 21 Allen Jovica. Head Coach Dave Randall, Assistant Ian Sneddon, Staff Stefan Regnier.

ALBERTA CUP FINAL	PROVINCIAL WINNERS	SCORE	RUNNERS UP
2007-09-03 Edmonton, AB	Calgary Caledonian FC	W 1-0 L	Calgary Villains Elite
CS NATIONAL CHAMPIONSHIPS	**GROUP WINNERS**	**SCORE**	**OPPONENT**
2007-10-03 Halifax, NS	Calgary Caledonian FC	W 4-1 L	St. Lawrence Laurentiens
2007-10-04 Halifax, NS	Calgary Caledonian FC	D 0-0 D	Fred. Picaroons Reds
2007-10-05 Halifax, NS	Calgary Caledonian FC	W 2-0 L	Panellinios Montréal FC
2007-10-06 Halifax, NS	Calgary Caledonian FC	W 2-0 L	Cornwall Eliot River
CHALLENGE TROPHY FINAL	**CHAMPIONS**	**SCORE**	**RUNNERS UP**
2007-10-08 Halifax, NS	Calgary Caledonian FC	W 5-0 L	Vancouver Columbus FC

Calgary's goals in the Final were scored by Mark Slade (three), Cenek Patik and Nicky Reyes.
Most Valuable Player of the Men's National Championships : Mark Slade.

— CHALLENGE TROPHY

2008 Calgary Caledonian FC
FOURTH NATIONAL CHAMPIONSHIP

MONDAY 13 OCTOBER 2008 - KING GEORGE V PARK IN ST. JOHN'S

Callies won their fourth Canadian title

Calgary Caledonian FC won their fourth Challenge Trophy in 10 years when they beat Corfinium St-Léonard at Canada Soccer's 2008 National Championships. Nicky Reyes, Mark Slade and Steffen Holdt were the goalscorers as the Callies won 3-1 at historic King George V Park in St. John's.

Holdt was later named Most Valuable Player of the 2008 National Championships. Both Holdt and Brett Colvin co-led the Callies with three goals each across the tournament.

Before winning the National Championships, Calgary Caledonian FC won the 2008 Alberta Cup provincial championship in their hometown during Labour Day weekend. During the season, they won their fifth-straight Alberta Major Soccer League title (their ninth league title in 11 years).

CHAMPIONS : CALGARY CALEDONIAN FC (CALLIES)

2008 Calgary Caledonian FC (unknown lineup for the Final) : 0 GK Dave Harrison, 0 GK Will Langford; Allen Jovica, 2 Ben Duffy, 3 Drew Milne, 4 Cenek Patik, 5 André Duberry, 6 Eric Roa, 7 Nicky Reyes, 8 Jamie Auvigne, 9 Mark Slade, 10 Steffen Holdt, 11 Felix Napuri, 12 Liam De Silva, 13 Francisco Miron, 14 Cody Cook, 16 Santino Gaetano, 17 Brett Colvin, 19 Milan Timotijevic, 20 Chris Kooy. Head Coach Dave Randall, Assistant Iain Sneddon, Team Manager Scott Sneddon, Staff Stefan Regnier.

ALBERTA CUP FINAL	PROVINCIAL WINNERS	SCORE	RUNNERS UP
2008-09-01 Calgary, AB	Calgary Caledonian FC D	0-0	D Edmonton Green & Gold

Calgary won 4-1 on kicks from the penalty mark.

CS NATIONAL CHAMPIONSHIPS	GROUP WINNERS	SCORE	OPPONENT
2008-10-08 St. John's, NL	Calgary Caledonian FC W	2-1	L Avondale Islanders
2008-10-09 St. John's, NL	Calgary Caledonian FC W	2-0	L Yorkton United
2008-10-10 St. John's, NL	Calgary Caledonian FC W	4-3	L Halifax City SC
2008-10-11 St. John's, NL	Calgary Caledonian FC W	3-1	L Winnipeg Hellas SC

CHALLENGE TROPHY FINAL	CHAMPIONS	SCORE	RUNNERS UP
2008-10-13 St. John's, NL	Calgary Caledonian FC W	3-1	L Corfinium St-Léonard

Calgary's goals in the Final were scored by Nicky Reyes, Mark Slade and Steffen Holdt.
Most Valuable Player of the Men's National Championships : Steffen Holdt.

CHALLENGE TROPHY

Winnipeg Hellas SC
FIRST NATIONAL CHAMPIONSHIP

MONDAY 12 OCTOBER 2009 - SASKTEL FIELD HOUSE IN SASKATOON

Winnipeg went indoors to win first title

Winnipeg Hellas SC won Canada Soccer's 2009 National Championships after they beat Royal-Sélect Beauport by a single goal in the Canadian Final. Chris Musto scored the match winner while teen goalkeeper Dylan O'Connor and his backline posted the clean sheet.

After the first day of the competition was played outdoors at multiple venues in the snow, the last five days were all played indoors at the SaskTel Field House. With a congested schedule and only one indoor venue, all remaining matches were limited to just 60 minutes each (including the Canadian Final).

Hellas SC had their big day in the snow when they beat the two-time national champions Calgary Callies on the opening day.

Before winning the 2009 National Championships, Winnipeg Hellas SC captured the Manitoba Cup provincial championship with a 1-0 victory after Lucania scored on their own goal.

CHAMPIONS : WINNIPEG HELLAS SC
2009 Winnipeg Hellas SC: 29 GK Dylan O'Connor; 6 Billy Economou, 11 Edin Kurbegovic (18 Justin Castalanos), 16 Tom Foderaro, 19 Andry Giesbrecht (13 Chris Musto, 14 Ulrick Disna), 5 Dimitri Ifandis (7 Vinny Ferlaino), 3 Tim Mullen, 17 Jeff Valdivia, 8 Thomas Findlay, 10 Trevor Perrault (21 Jorge Mendez), 12 Jordan Goetting. Did not feature in the Final: 1 GK Kyle Kilcup; 2 Phillip Porpiglia, 9 Fabio Capone, 20 Yiannis Isalatsidis. Head Coach Kostas Vailas, Team Manager Angelo Charalabopoulos, Trainer Andrée Anne Carrière, President George Ifandis.

MANITOBA CUP FINAL	PROVINCIAL WINNERS	SCORE		RUNNERS UP
2009-08-15 Winnipeg, MB	Winnipeg Hellas SC	W 1-0	L	Winnipeg Lucania SC
CS NATIONAL CHAMPIONSHIPS	**GROUP WINNERS**	**SCORE**		**OPPONENT**
2009-10-07 Saskatoon, SK	Winnipeg Hellas SC	W 2-1	L	Calgary Caledonian FC
2009-10-08 Saskatoon, SK	Winnipeg Hellas SC	W 1-0	L	West Van FC
2009-10-10 Saskatoon, SK	Winnipeg Hellas SC	L 0-3	W	Sask. Huskie Alumni
2009-10-11 Saskatoon, SK	Winnipeg Hellas SC	W 2-0	L	Real Toronto FC
CHALLENGE TROPHY FINAL	**CHAMPIONS**	**SCORE**		**RUNNERS UP**
2009-10-12 Saskatoon, SK	Winnipeg Hellas SC	W 1-0	L	Royal-Sélect Beauport

Winnipeg's lone goal in the Final was scored by Chris Musto.

CANADIAN SOCCER HISTORY
MEN'S AMATEUR FOOTBALL CHAMPIONS

2010s

■ CHALLENGE TROPHY

2010 *Charlottetown Abbies*
FIRST NATIONAL CHAMPIONSHIP

MONDAY 11 OCTOBER 2010 - UNIVERSITY OF PEI IN CHARLOTTETOWN
Norton scored PEI winner in extra time

Charlottetown Abbies SC Churchill Arms became the first Prince Edward Island club to win Canada Soccer's National Championships when they beat Victoria Gorge FC in the 2010 Canadian Final. Brett Norton and Ryan Anstey both scored in the second period of extra time as the PEI club won the National Championships in their hometown.

Goalkeeper Matt Lally finished the tournament with four clean sheets in four matches. In the group phase, they won 2-0 over Holy Cross FC, won 1-0 over Halifax Dunbrack SC, drew 0-0 with Royal-Sélect Beauport, and won 1-0 over PEI Selects (with Andrew MacCormack in goal).

Before winning the 2010 National Championships, Charlottetown won the two-leg PEI Cup provincial championship against the younger Prince Edward Island Selects.

CHAMPIONS : CHARLOTTETOWN ABBIES SC

2010 Charlottetown PEI FC / Charlottetown Abbies SC Churchill Arms : 1 GK Matt Lally; 2 Rob Aiken, 4 Graham Ashworth, 6 Jonathan Vos captain, 7 Dylan MacDonald, 8 Matt Thomson, 10 Ryan Anstey, 14 Paul Craig, 15 Michel Daoust-Wheatley, 16 Brett Norton, 20 Karel Prickett. Alternates: 3 Jared Murphy, 9 Jordan Chandler, 11 Nathan Beck, 17 Dan McAleer, 19 Kenny Morrison, 29 Josh Vessey, 51 Russell Carson. Did not feature in the Final: 13 GK Andrew MacCormack, 12 Nathan Snowie (injured). Head Coach John Diamond, Assistant Bruce Norton, Staff Lewis Page, Staff David Snowie.

PEI CUP FINAL	PROVINCIAL WINNERS	SCORE	RUNNERS UP
2010-08-22 Charlottetown, PE	Charlottetown Abbies	2-1	PEI Selects
2010-08-25 Charlottetown, PE	Charlottetown Abbies	1-0	PEI Selects
CS NATIONAL CHAMPIONSHIPS	**GROUP WINNERS**	**SCORE**	**OPPONENT**
2010-10-06 Charlottetown, PE	Charlottetown Abbies W	2-0	L Holy Cross FC
2010-10-07 Charlottetown, PE	Charlottetown Abbies W	1-0	L Halifax Dunbrack SC
2010-10-08 Charlottetown, PE	Charlottetown Abbies D	0-0	D Royal-Sélect Beauport
2010-10-10 Charlottetown, PE	Charlottetown Abbies W	1-0	L PEI Selects
CHALLENGE TROPHY FINAL	**CHAMPIONS**	**SCORE**	**RUNNERS UP**
2010-10-11 Charlottetown, PE	Charlottetown Abbies W	2-0	L Victoria Gorge FC

Charlottetown's goals in the Final were scored in extra time by Brett Norton and Ryan Anstey.

Saskatoon HUSA Alumni
FIRST NATIONAL CHAMPIONSHIP

MONDAY 10 OCTOBER 2011 - ILLINOIS IN BROSSARD, QUÉBEC
Saskatoon HUSA Alumni won 2011 title

Saskatoon HUSA Alumni became the first Saskatchewan club to win Canada Soccer's National Championships when they beat Surrey ICST Pegasus in the 2011 Canadian Final. Nathan Reis and Mitchell Collins scored the goals while goalkeeper Jeff Dobchuk posted the clean sheet for the 2-0 win.

Across the tournament, Dobchuk posted three clean sheets in four matches while Mark Korthius led the team with four goals in five matches.

Saskatoon actually lost to Surrey in the group phase, but both teams advanced to the Quarterfinals. After a 4-0 win over Suburban FC in the Quarterfinals, Saskatoon reached the Canadian Final after they beat Toronto Celtic 2-1 in the Semifinals.

Before winning the National Championships, Saskatoon HUSA Alumni won the 2011 Saskatchewan provincial championship after they finished at the top of a four-team, round-robin series in Saskatoon. It was their third-straight provincial title.

CHAMPIONS : SASKATOON HUSA ALUMNI
2011 Saskatoon HUSA Alumni : 1 GK Jeff Dobchuk, 2 Stephen Patterson, 3 Brendan Garritty, 4 Jordan Schidlowsky, 5 Ryan McAllister, 8 Nathan Reis, 9 Jarvis Huyghebaert, 17 Jeff Friesen, 18 Mark Korthuis, 19 Jay Tomchuk, 21 Dwayne Gareau. Alernates: 30 GK Mitchell Cantin, 7 Jamie Hembroff, 12 Steven Irinici, 14 Michael Veszi, 15 David Patterson, 16 Michael Collins, 20 David Brown. Head Coach Stewart Gillott, Staff Sherren Gillott.

CS NATIONAL CHAMPIONSHIPS	GROUP STAGE	SCORE	OPPONENT
2011-10-06 Brossard, QC	Saskatoon HUSA Alumni W	4-0 L	Fred. Picaroons Reds
2011-10-07 Brossard, QC	Saskatoon HUSA Alumni L	1-2 W	Surrey ICST Pegasus
CS QUARTERFINALS & SEMIFINALS	**WINNERS**	**SCORE**	**OPPONENT**
2011-10-08 Brossard, QC	Saskatoon HUSA Alumni W	4-0 L	Suburban FC
2011-10-09 Brossard, QC	Saskatoon HUSA Alumni W	2-1 L	Toronto Celtic
CHALLENGE TROPHY FINAL	**CHAMPIONS**	**SCORE**	**RUNNERS UP**
2011-10-10 Brossard, QC	Saskatoon HUSA Alumni W	2-0 L	Surrey ICST Pegasus

Saskatoon's goals in the Final were scored by Nathan Reis and Mitchell Collins.

■ CHALLENGE TROPHY ■

2012 Royal-Sélect Beauport
FIRST NATIONAL CHAMPIONSHIP

MONDAY 8 OCTOBER 2012 - WINNIPEG SPORTS COMPLEX

Le Royal won on kicks after 3-3 thriller

Royal-Sélect Beauport captured Canada Soccer's 2012 National Championships after they beat Edmonton Scottish SC in a shootout at the Winnipeg Sports Complex. It was a memorable Canadian Final that ended 3-3 after 120 minutes before Beauport won 4-2 on kicks from the penalty mark.

Midfielder Samuel Georget was named the Most Valuable Player of the National Championships after he led Beauport with five goals in five matches. Georget (his brilliant 1-1 equaliser), Nafi Dicko-Raynaud (2-1) and Vincent Barrette (3-3) were the Beauport goalscorers in the Final.

Before winning the National Championships, Royal-Sélect Beauport captured the 2012 Québec Cup after they won 3-2 over the Rapides de Chaudière-Ouest.

CHAMPIONS : ROYAL-SÉLECT BEAUPORT

2012 Royal-Sélect Beauport : 1 GK Vincent Cournoyer; 2 Omar Gutierrez, 4 Nafi Dicko-Raynauld, 5 Jamel Berbèche, 6 Augustin Mangaïko, 7 Guillaume Héroux, 10 Samuel Georget, 11 Patrice Dion, 13 Lawrence Hone-Blanchet, 14 Michel Mana Nga captain, 15 Pascal Bragagnolo. Substitutions featured: 3 Vincent Barrette, 8 Eduardo Davalos, 12 Jimmy McLachlan, 18 Boris Salou, 19 Julien Mbonyineza, 20 Guillaume Barrette. Did not feature in the Final: 22 GK Jean-François Desrosiers, 16 Goran Rimac, 17 Michaël Boutin. Manager Samir Ghrib.

COUPE DU QUÉBEC	PROVINCIAL WINNERS	SCORE	OPPONENT
2012-09-02 Laval, QC	Royal-Sélect Beauport	W 3-2 L	Chaudière-Ouest
CS NATIONAL CHAMPIONSHIPS	**GROUP STAGE**	**SCORE**	**OPPONENT**
2012-10-04 Winnipeg, MB	Royal-Sélect Beauport	W 4-0 L	Yellowknife FC
2012-10-05 Winnipeg, MB	Royal-Sélect Beauport	W 2-0 L	AEK London FC
CS QUARTERFINALS & SEMIFINALS	**WINNERS**	**SCORE**	**OPPONENT**
2012-10-06 Winnipeg, MB	Royal-Sélect Beauport	W 4-0 L	Surrey Utd. Firefighters
2012-10-07 Winnipeg, MB	Royal-Sélect Beauport	W 2-1 L	PEI FC
CHALLENGE TROPHY FINAL	**CHAMPIONS**	**SCORE**	**RUNNERS UP**
2012-10-08 Winnipeg, MB	Royal-Sélect Beauport	D 3-3 D	Edmonton Scottish SC

Beauport's goals in the Final were scored by Samuel Georget, Nafi Dicko-Raynaud and Vincent Barrette. After the 3-3 draw, Beauport won 4-2 on kicks from the penalty mark.
Most Valuable Player of the Men's National Championships : Samuel Georget.

— CHALLENGE TROPHY —

Gloucester Celtic FC
FIRST NATIONAL CHAMPIONSHIP

MONDAY 14 OCTOBER 2013 - MAINLAND COMMONS IN HALIFAX

Gulliver scored brace as Celtic won title

Ottawa's Gloucester Celtic FC captured Canada Soccer's 2013 National Championships after they won 3-0 over Surrey United Firefighters in the Canadian Final. Ryne Gulliver (two) and Alex Walker were the Gloucester goalscorers while goalkeeper Matt Gagnon posted the clean sheet.

Centre back Tom MacDonald was named the Most Valuable Player of the National Championships and Gloucester Celtic were perfect 4-0-0 with him in the lineup (he played four of Gloucester's five matches in Halifax). MacDonald helped Gloucester post three consecutive clean sheets in the knockout phase from the Quarterfinals to the Canadian Final.

Gloucester were only beaten by the 2011 national champions Saskatoon HUSA Alumni in the group phase.

Before winning the 2013 National Championships, Gloucester Celtic FC captured the Ontario Cup with a 3-2 victory over Caledon SC.

CHAMPIONS : GLOUCESTER CELTIC FC

2013 Gloucester Celtic FC : 1 GK Matt Gagnon; 2 Adam Davies, 4 Andrew Park, 7 Matt Quon, 8 Jason DaCosta, 9 Josh Dewar, 11 Tom MacDonald, 17 Colin Roberts, 21 Justin Dasah, 28 Bezick Evraire, 41 Phil Sangster. Substitutions featured: 13 Alex DeCouvreur, 14 Warwick Sangster, 15 Alex Walker, 18 Panagiotis Manginas, 24 Ryne Gulliver, 80 Emmanuel Desjeunes. Did not feature in the Final: 3 Roberto Gutierrez, 6 Jorge Gulierrez. Manager Matt Williams, Assistant Ryan Lauzon.

ONTARIO CUP FINAL	PROVINCIAL WINNERS	SCORE	RUNNERS UP
2013-09-15 Oshawa, ON	Gloucester Celtic FC	W 3-2	L Caledon SC
CS NATIONAL CHAMPIONSHIPS	**GROUP STAGE**	**SCORE**	**OPPONENT**
2013-10-10 Halifax, NS	Gloucester Celtic FC	W 4-1	L Fredericton Wanderers
2013-10-11 Halifax, NS	Gloucester Celtic FC	L 0-2	W Saskatoon HUSA Alumni
CS QUARTERFINALS & SEMIFINALS	**WINNERS**	**SCORE**	**OPPONENT**
2013-10-12 Halifax, NS	Gloucester Celtic FC	W 1-0	L Halifax City SC
2013-10-13 Halifax, NS	Gloucester Celtic FC	W 1-0	L FC Winnipeg Lions
CHALLENGE TROPHY FINAL	**CHAMPIONS**	**SCORE**	**RUNNERS UP**
2013-10-14 Halifax, NS	Gloucester Celtic FC	W 3-0	L Surrey Utd. Firefighters

Gloucester's goals in the Final were scored by Ryne Gulliver (two) and Alex Walker.
Most Valuable Player of the Men's National Championships : Tom MacDonald.

– CHALLENGE TROPHY

2014 London Marconi SC
FIRST NATIONAL CHAMPIONSHIP

MONDAY 13 OCTOBER 2014 - ONTARIO SOCCER CENTRE IN VAUGHAN

London won 4-2 on kicks to capture title

London Marconi SC captured Canada Soccer's National Championships for the first time when they beat the Calgary Callies in a shootout in the 2014 Canadian Final. The two sides played to a scoreless draw before London won 4-2 on kicks from the penalty mark.

Denver Spearman was named Most Valuable Player of the National Championships after he played every minute of London's title run across five matches in Vaughan. Goalkeeper Mark Haynes posted three clean sheets in five matches, including the 1-0 win over FC Winnipeg Lions in the Semifinals and the 0-0 draw in the Canadian Final.

Before winning the 2014 National Championships, London Marconi SC captured the Ontario Cup provincial championship with a 3-1 victory over Vaughan Azzurri. It was London Marconi's first Ontario Cup title since 1978.

CHAMPIONS : LONDON MARCONI SC
2014 London Marconi SC : 1 GK Mark Haynes, 2 Ryan Avola, 3 Brandon Mendes, 4 Alex Lewis, 5 Tyler Hemming, 8 Connor McFall, 9 Taso Bujouves, 13 Denver Spearman, 15 Jovan Ivanovich, 17 Brian Pistor, 22 Matt Catalano. Substitutions featured: 6 Aaron Schneebeli, 8 Connor McFall, 11 Paul Arnold, 12 Birani Ahmed, 18 Geert Remjin. Did not feature: 7 Steven Hepton, 20 Matthew Cuthbert. Head Coach Pat McLaughlin, Assistant Ugo DeCandido, Staff Tom Kouzounas, Staff John Alcatrao.

ONTARIO CUP FINAL	PROVINCIAL WINNERS	SCORE	RUNNERS UP
2014-09-14 Oshawa, ON	London Marconi SC W	3-1	L Vaughan Azzurri
CS NATIONAL CHAMPIONSHIPS	**GROUP STAGE**	**SCORE**	**OPPONENT**
2014-10-08 Vaughan, ON	London Marconi SC D	0-0	D Vaughan Azzurri
2014-10-10 Vaughan, ON	London Marconi SC W	3-1	L PEI FC
CS QUARTERFINALS & SEMIFINALS	**WINNERS**	**SCORE**	**OPPONENT**
2014-10-11 Vaughan, ON	London Marconi SC D	2-2	D Holy Cross FC
London won on kicks from the penalty mark.			
2014-10-12 Vaughan, ON	London Marconi SC W	1-0	L FC Winnipeg Lions
CHALLENGE TROPHY FINAL	**CHAMPIONS**	**SCORE**	**RUNNERS UP**
2014-10-13 Vaughan, ON	London Marconi SC D	0-0	D Calgary Caledonian FC

After the 0-0 draw, London Marconi SC won 4-2 on kicks from the penalty mark.
Most Valuable Player of the Men's National Championships : Denver Spearman.

London Marconi SC

SECOND NATIONAL CHAMPIONSHIP

MONDAY 12 OCTOBER 2015 - CALGARY SOCCER CENTRE

Ivanovich scored winner in extra time

London Marconi SC won their second-straight Challenge Trophy in 2015 when they beat Edmonton Scottish SC in extra time at Canada Soccer's National Championships. Jovan Ivanovich was the hero after he scored the 2-1 match winner in extra time.

Ivanovich earned Man of the Match honours in the Canadian Final and he was named Most Valuable Player of the National Championships. He scored the 1-0 opener in the Canadian Final before Edmonton equalised late in the second half. He scored the match winner in the 114th minute.

London Marconi SC were the first back-to-back Challenge Trophy winners since the Calgary Callies won Canadian amateur titles in 2007 and 2008.

Before winning the 2015 National Championships, London Marconi SC captured the Ontario Cup with a 5-0 victory over Mississauga Portofino.

CHAMPIONS : LONDON MARCONI SC

2015 London Marconi SC : 1 GK Mark Haynes, 2 Ryan Avola, 5 Tyler Hemming, 6 Alex Lewis, 7 Denver Spearman, 8 Michael Pereira, 11 Younan Samra, 15 Jovan Ivanovich, 10 Connor McFall, 22 Matt Catalano, 24 Anthony Perez. Substitutions featured: 4 Aaron Schneebeli, 9 Geert Remjin, 12 Ahmad Birani, 20 Paul Arnold. Did not feature in the Final: 3 Alex Blencowe, 16 Luke Jackson, 19 Mike Mracoccia, 25 GK Igor Kasic. Head Coach Pat McLaughlin, Assistant Ugo DeCandido, Staff Tom Kouzounas, Staff John Alcatrao.

ONTARIO CUP FINAL	PROVINCIAL WINNERS	SCORE	RUNNERS UP
2015-09-12 Vaughan, ON	London Marconi SC	W 5-0 L	Mississauga Portofino
CS NATIONAL CHAMPIONSHIPS	**GROUP WINNERS**	**SCORE**	**OPPONENT**
2015-10-07 Calgary, AB	London Marconi SC	W 1-0 L	Chaudière-Ouest
2015-10-09 Calgary, AB	London Marconi SC	W 2-0 L	PEI FC
CS QUARTERFINALS & SEMIFINALS	**WINNERS**	**SCORE**	**OPPONENT**
2015-10-10 Calgary, AB	London Marconi SC	W 2-0 L	Holy Cross FC
2015-10-11 Calgary, AB	London Marconi SC	W 2-0 L	EDC FC Burnaby
CHALLENGE TROPHY FINAL	**CHAMPIONS**	**SCORE**	**RUNNERS UP**
2015-10-12 Calgary, AB	London Marconi SC	W 2-1 L	Edmonton Scottish SC

London's goals in the Final were both scored by Jovan Ivanovich.
Most Valuable Player of the Men's National Championships : Jovan Ivanovich.

■ CHALLENGE TROPHY

2016 Edmonton Scottish SC
FIRST NATIONAL CHAMPIONSHIP

MONDAY 10 OCTOBER 2016 - KING GEORGE V PARK IN ST. JOHN'S
Wheeler scored Edmonton's late winner

Edmonton Scottish SC finally won Canada Soccer's Challenge Trophy in 2016 when they beat 2012 winners Royal-Sélect Beauport at the National Championships in St. John's. Steven Wheeler was the hero when he scored the 1-0 match winner three minutes into added time.

Edmonton Scottish SC were previously national runners up in 1972, 2012 and 2015. They lost the 2012 Canadian Final to Beauport.

Captain Paul Hamilton was named the Most Valuable Player of the 2016 National Championships. The Edmonton centre back helped his team post five-straight clean sheets in six days.

Before winning the National Championships, Edmonton Scottish SC captured the 2016 Alberta Cup in Edmonton during Labour Day weekend. During the season, they won Alberta Major Soccer League men's division.

CHAMPIONS : EDMONTON SCOTTISH SC
2016 Edmonton Scottish SC : 1 GK Jay Vetsch (1 GK Francisco Wong); 4 Michael McCormick, 18 Paul Hamilton captain, 19 James Carr, 15 Anoop Sahota; 20 Chris Kooy, 8 John Pegg (16 Nicky Reyes), 10 Chris Lemire; 7 Sam Lam; 11 Almir Gazic (9 Marcus Johnstone), 14 Dexter McLachlan (13 Steve Wheeler). Did not feature in the Final: 3 Karim Broodhagen, 5 Richard Klein, 6 Nicolas Gonzalez (injured), 12 Christian Kosmin, 21 Dave Rutledge. Head Coach Kevin Poissant, Assistant Miles Hunt, Staff Cathy Vetsch, Staff James Black.

ALBERTA CUP FINAL	PROVINCIAL WINNERS	SCORE	RUNNERS UP
2016-09-05 Edmonton, AB	Edmonton Scottish SC	W 2-1 L	Edmonton Green & Gold
CS NATIONAL CHAMPIONSHIPS	**GROUP STAGE**	**SCORE**	**OPPONENT**
2016-10-05 St. John's, NL	Edmonton Scottish SC	W 1-0 L	Western Halifax FC
2016-10-07 Mount Pearl, NL	Edmonton Scottish SC	W 3-0 L	Fred. Picaroons Reds
CS QUARTERFINALS & SEMIFINALS	**WINNERS**	**SCORE**	**OPPONENT**
2016-10-08 Mount Pearl, NL	Edmonton Scottish SC	W 2-0 L	Edmonton Green & Gold
2016-10-09 St. John's, NL	Edmonton Scottish SC	W 2-0 L	Saskatoon HUSA Alumni
CHALLENGE TROPHY FINAL	**CHAMPIONS**	**SCORE**	**RUNNERS UP**
2016-10-10 St. John's, NL	Edmonton Scottish SC	W 1-0 L	Royal-Sélect Beauport

Edmonton's lone goal in the Final was scored by Steven Wheeler.
Most Valuable Player of the Men's National Championships : centre back Paul Hamilton.

CHALLENGE TROPHY

Western Halifax FC
FIRST NATIONAL CHAMPIONSHIP

MONDAY 9 OCTOBER 2017 - NEWTON ATHLETIC PARK IN SURREY
MacRae scored early match winner

Western Halifax FC won Canada Soccer's 2017 National Championships when they beat FC Winnipeg Lions by a single goal in the Canadian Final. That goal was scored by Calum MacRae in the third minute after which neither team could beat the goalkeepers. Christian Oxner got the clean sheet for Halifax.

Jhonattan Córdoba earned Man of the Match honours in the Canadian Final and he was named the Most Valuable Player of the 2017 National Championships. He led Western Halifax FC with three goals in five matches.

Before winning the 2017 National Championships, Western Halifax FC captured the Nova Scotia provincial championship after they beat Halifax City SC in a shootout. After a 2-2 draw, Western Halifax FC won 4-2 on kicks from the penalty mark.

CHAMPIONS : WESTERN HALIFAX FC
2017 Western Halifax FC : 50 GK Christian Oxner; 2 Matt Cousens, 3 Pawel Gorski, 7 Danny LeBlanc, 9 Calum MacRae, 10 Jhonattan Córdoba, 11 Wes Hawley, 13 Shane Rajaraman captain, 14 Leo Sanchez, 21 James Nearing, 24 Jeff Arkin. Substitutions featured: 8 Alex Córdoba, 22 James Matthews. Did not feature in the Final: 1 Gk Tristan Leopold, 5 Shawn Kodejs captain (injured), 16 Quinn Park (injured), 23 Jack Schembri. Head Coach Alan Jazic, Team Manager Mridula McGuinness. Did not travel: 12 Michael Trim, 18 Jonny Doucett.

NOVA SCOTIA CUP FINAL	PROVINCIAL WINNERS	SCORE		RUNNERS UP
2017-08-22 Halifax, NS	Western Halifax FC	D 2-2	D	Halifax City SC
Western Halifax FC won 4-2 on kicks from the penalty mark.				
CS NATIONAL CHAMPIONSHIPS	**GROUP WINNERS**	**SCORE**		**OPPONENT**
2017-10-05 Surrey, BC	Western Halifax FC	W 3-1	L	Holy Cross FC
2017-10-06 Surrey, BC	Western Halifax FC	W 2-0	L	Calgary Caledonian FC
2017-10-07 Surrey, BC	Western Halifax FC	W 2-1	L	Vancouver Club Inter FC
2017-10-08 Surrey, BC	Western Halifax FC	D 1-1	D	Saskatoon HUSA Alumni
CHALLENGE TROPHY FINAL	**CHAMPIONS**	**SCORE**		**RUNNERS UP**
2017-10-09 Surrey, BC	Western Halifax FC	W 1-0	L	FC Winnipeg Lions

Halifax's lone goal in the Final scored by Calum MacRae.
Most Valuable Player of the Men's National Championships : Jhonattan Córdoba.

2018 Surrey BC Tigers Hurricanes
FIRST NATIONAL CHAMPIONSHIP

MONDAY 8 OCTOBER 2018 - UMEA FIELD IN SASKATOON

Soolsma scored four goals in Surrey win

Surrey BC Tigers Hurricanes captured Canada Soccer's 2018 National Championships in Saskatoon after they won 7-3 over Caledon SC of Ontario. Former professional Nick Soolsma led the way with four goals while teammates Ryan Dhillon (two) and Pavi Dhillon also scored for Surrey.

Soolsma earned Man of the Match honours in the Canadian Final and he was named the Most Valuable Player of the National Championships. He led the tournament with nine goals in five matches. Soolsma was the seventh player in the history of the competition to score a hat trick on the last day of the Canadian Final.

Before winning the 2018 National Championships, Surrey BC Tigers Hurricanes captured the BC Province Cup with a 5-2 victory over Langley United at Burnaby's Swangard Stadium. MVP Soolsma scored a hat trick in the provincial championship.

CHAMPIONS : SURREY BC TIGERS HURRICANES

2018 Surrey BC Tigers Hurricanes : 27 GK Surrey BC Tigers Hurricanes Sandhu; 3 Arjan Grewal (15 Gary Badesha), 5 Jason Gill captain (2 Jesse Dhami), 6 Ryan Ashlee, 12 Ryan Dhillon; 8 Sarpeet Pahal (21 David Chohan), 23 Cam Hundal, 10 Harpreet Khakh (16 Jeevi Rai), 11 Daniel Davidson (9 Navjot Thind, 11 Ashif Ismail), 18 Nicky Soolsma, 7 Pavi Dhillon (13 Joey Brar). Did not feature in the Final: 17 William Bundy, 24 Gurjot Lehal. Head Coach Satbir Badesha, Assistant Robert Jandric, Staff Inderpaul Khaira.

BC PROVINCE CUP FINAL	PROVINCIAL WINNERS	SCORE		RUNNERS UP
2018-05-13 Burnaby, BC	Surrey BC Tigers Hurricanes	W 5-2	L	Langley United
CS NATIONAL CHAMPIONSHIPS	**GROUP WINNERS**	**SCORE**		**OPPONENT**
2018-10-03 Saskatoon, SK	Surrey BC Tigers Hurricanes	D 1-1	D	Saskatoon Revolution
2018-10-04 Saskatoon, SK	Surrey BC Tigers Hurricanes	W 3-2	L	Edmonton Scottish SC
2018-10-06 Saskatoon, SK	Surrey BC Tigers Hurricanes	W 2-1	L	Western Halifax FC
2018-10-07 Saskatoon, SK	Surrey BC Tigers Hurricanes	W 4-0	L	Fred. Picaroons Reds
CHALLENGE TROPHY FINAL	**CHAMPIONS**	**SCORE**		**RUNNERS UP**
2018-10-08 Saskatoon, SK	Surrey BC Tigers Hurricanes	W 7-3	L	Caledon SC

Surrey's goals in the Final scored by Ryan Dhillon (two), Pavi Dhillon, Nick Soolsma (four).
Most Valuable Player of the Men's National Championships : Nick Soolsma.

CHALLENGE TROPHY

Surrey Central City Breakers
FIRST NATIONAL CHAMPIONSHIP

 2019

MONDAY 14 OCTOBER 2019 - KING GEORGE V PARK IN ST. JOHN'S

CCB kept Canadian honours in Surrey

Surrey's Central City Breakers won Canada Soccer's 2019 National Championships after they beat Ottawa St. Anthony SC in the Canadian Final. Caleb Clarke and Milad Mehrabi scored the goals while goalkeeper Luke O'Shea posted the clean sheet for the 2-0 victory at King George V Park in St. John's.

Veteran midfielder Bobby Jhutty was named the Most Valuable Player of the National Championships while forward Milad Mehrabi earned Man of the Match honours in the Canadian Final. Clarke and Mehrabi co-led the Breakers with four goals each.

Before winning the 2019 National Championships, the Central City Breakers won the BC Province Cup with a 4-1 victory over FC Tigers Vancouver. Caleb Clarke scored twice in the British Columbia provincial championship.

CHAMPIONS : SURREY CENTRAL CITY BREAKERS FC

2019 Surrey Central City Breakers FC : 1 GK Luke O'Shea captain; 3 Brendan Campbell, 4 Andres Romo, 6 Mamadi Camara (13 Kalem Scott), 7 Harry Lakhan, 9 Milad Mehrabi (9 Milad Rahmati), 10 Bobby Jhutty, 11 Boris Si, 14 Caleb Clarke, 22 Nicolas Morello, 23 Yassin Essa (15 Ajeet Bains). Did not feature in the Final: 0 GK Arash Shirazi, 2 Shane Satar, 5 Derrick Bassi, 8 Dzenan Rezdrob, 12 Andy Phillips, 16 Amir Amiry. Manager Ted Hans, Coach Diaz Kambero, Assistant Peter Malakoane, Assistant Danoosh Askarpoor, Staff Garry Sangha.

BC PROVINCE CUP FINAL	PROVINCIAL WINNERS	SCORE	RUNNERS UP
2019-05 12 Nanaimo, BC	Surrey Central City Breakers	W 4-1	L FC Tigers Vancouver
CS NATIONAL CHAMPIONSHIPS	**GROUP WINNERS**	**SCORE**	**OPPONENT**
2019-10-09 Mount Pearl, NL	Surrey Central City Breakers	W 2-1	L FC Winnipeg Lions
2019-10-10 St. John's, NL	Surrey Central City Breakers	W 2-1	L Holy Cross FC
2019-10-11 Mount Pearl, NL	Surrey Central City Breakers	W 4-0	L Fred. Picaroons Reds
2019-10-12 Mount Pearl, NL	Surrey Central City Breakers	D 1-1	D Edmonton Scottish SC
CHALLENGE TROPHY FINAL	**CHAMPIONS**	**SCORE**	**RUNNERS UP**
2019-10-14 St. John's, NL	Surrey Central City Breakers	W 2-0	L Ottawa St. Anthony SC

Surrey's goals in the Final scored by Caleb Clarke and Milad Mehrabi.
Most Valuable Player of the Men's National Championships : Bhupinder "Bobby" Jhutty.

CANADIAN SOCCER HISTORY
MEN'S AMATEUR FOOTBALL CHAMPIONS

THE NEW DECADE

2022 Gloucester Celtic FC
SECOND NATIONAL CHAMPIONSHIP

MONDAY 10 OCTOBER 2022 - NORTH MAPLE IN VAUGHAN, ONTARIO
Gloucester Celtic won their second title

Ottawa's Gloucester Celtic FC won their second Challenge Trophy after they scored a pair of first-half goals against Edmonton Green & Gold in the first National Championships since the global pandemic. Kieran Sanders and Andrew Bryan were the goalscorers as Celtic won 2-0 in the 2022 Canadian Final.

Forward Bezick Evraire was named the Most Valuable Player of the National Championships after he scored two goals and four assists in four matches. Gloucester and Holy Cross FC had actually finished tied on points in the group phase, but Gloucester advanced to the Canadian Final with the better goals difference.

Before winning the 2022 National Championships, Gloucester Celtic FC captured the Ontario Cup provincial championship with a 3-1 victory over Caledon SC. Gloucester Celtic FC also won the 2021 Ontario Cup when there was no National Championships because of the global pandemic.

CHAMPIONS : GLOUCESTER CELTIC FC
2022 Gloucester Celtic FC : 1 GK Corey Herrington; 14 Cameron Butterfield, 18 Panagiotis Manginas, 17 Karl Bicamumpaka, 2 Adam Davies captain; 10 Olivier Babineau, 7 Kieran Sanders, 16 Nevello Yoseke, 28 Bezick Evraire-Chance; 12 Joey Kewin; 15 Andrew Bryan. Substitutions featured: 11 Kelvin Asabre, 13 Alex DeCouvreur, 21 Justin Dasah, 24 GK Félix Daigle, 33 Emmanuel Desjeunes. Did not feature in the Final: 6 Yale Chadsey, 8 Jethro Pang. Manager Matt Williams, Head Coach Phil Sangster, Coach Matt Gagnon, Staff Robert Murphy, Staff Andrew Park.

ONTARIO CUP FINAL	PROVINCIAL WINNERS	SCORE	RUNNERS UP
2022-09-10 Vaughan, ON	Gloucester Celtic FC	W 3-1	L Caledon SC
CS NATIONAL CHAMPIONSHIPS	**GROUP WINNERS**	**SCORE**	**OPPONENT**
2022-10-05 Vaughan, ON	Gloucester Celtic FC	W 4-0	L WC Royals FC
2022-10-06 Vaughan, ON	Gloucester Celtic FC	D 1-1	D Holy Cross FC
2022-10-08 Vaughan, ON	Gloucester Celtic FC	W 3-1	L Halifax Dunbrack SC
CHALLENGE TROPHY FINAL	**CHAMPIONS**	**SCORE**	**RUNNERS UP**
2022-10-10 Vaughan, ON	Gloucester Celtic FC	W 2-0	L Edmonton Green & Gold

Gloucester's goals in the Final were scored by Kieran Sanders and Andrew Bryan.
Most Valuable Player of the Men's National Championships : Bezick Evraire.

West Ottawa SC
FIRST NATIONAL CHAMPIONSHIP  2023

MONDAY 9 OCTOBER 2023 - MAINLAND COMMONS IN HALIFAX

West Ottawa captured their first title

West Ottawa SC kept Canada Soccer's Challenge Trophy in the capital city after they won their first National Championships with a 1-0 victory over hosts Western Halifax FC in the 2023 Canadian Final. Ottawa's Zach El Shafei scored the lone goal in the 41st minute while goalkeeper Anton Favre posted the clean sheet.

Forward Javane Henry was named the Most Valuable Player of the National Championships while teen centre back Brady Curkovic earned Man of the Match honours in the Canadian Final. Malek Belhaj led the team with three goals in five matches.

Before winning the 2023 National Championships, West Ottawa SC captured the Ontario Cup provincial championship after they beat Scarborough GS United in a shootout. After a 2-2 draw, West Ottawa SC won 6-5 on kicks from the penalty mark.

CHAMPIONS : WEST OTTAWA SC

2023 West Ottawa SC : 0 GK Anton Favre; 4 Hasan Mohasar, 16 Isaac Johnson, 6 Brady Curkovic, 20 Emad Houache; 5 Daud Dahir (18 Michael Bastianelli), 23 Ricky Comba, 8 Sebastian Rodriguez captain, 9 Zach El Shafei (10 Marco Natoli); 15 Ayden Ayden (17 Malek Belhaj), 11 Javane Henry. Did not feature in Final: 1 GK Mitchell LeClair, 7 Mahir Hadziresic (injured), 12 Simon Rochon, 13 Jack Pensom (injured), 14 Matias Markus, 19 Owen McKee. Head Coach: Stephane Okane, Assistant Aakash Kapuria, Assistant Leonidas Legakis.

ONTARIO CUP FINAL	PROVINCIAL WINNERS	SCORE	RUNNERS UP
2023-09-10 Vaughan, ON	West Ottawa SC	D 2-2 D	Scarborough GS United
West Ottawa SC won 6-5 on kicks from the penalty mark.			
CS NATIONAL CHAMPIONSHIPS	**GROUP WINNERS**	**SCORE**	**OPPONENT**
2023-10-04 Halifax, NS	West Ottawa SC	W 2-1 L	Chaudière-Ouest
2023-10-05 Halifax, NS	West Ottawa SC	W 1-0 L	Surrey BB5 United
2023-10-06 Halifax, NS	West Ottawa SC	W 8-0 L	Fred. Picaroons Reds
2023-10-07 Halifax, NS	West Ottawa SC	L 1-3 W	FC Winnipeg Lions
CHALLENGE TROPHY FINAL	**CHAMPIONS**	**SCORE**	**RUNNERS UP**
2023-10-09 Halifax, NS	West Ottawa SC	W 1-0 L	Western Halifax FC

West Ottawa's goal in the Final was scored by Zach El Shafei.
Most Valuable Player of the Men's National Championships : Javane Henry.

CHAMPIONS

NORTH AMERICAN SOCCER FOOTBALL LEAGUE

PLAYOFF FINAL	NASFL CHAMPIONSHIP	RUNNERS UP
1946-09-21 Toronto, ON	Toronto Greenbacks SC won 3-0*	Detroit Wolverines FC

*Detroit did not want to play the second leg of the playoffs because they believed they were the champions on account of winning the regular season schedule

EASTERN CANADA PROFESSIONAL LEAGUE

LAST DAY of SEASON	LEAGUE CHAMPIONS	RUNNERS UP
1961-09-20 24 matches	Toronto City FC (11W-3D-10L)	Montréal Cantalia FC
1962-08-04 24 matches	Toronto Roma FC (12W-7D-5L)	Toronto City FC
1963-09-01 25 matches	Toronto Italia FC (19W-5D-1L)	Hamilton Steelers SC
1964-08-22 24 matches	Toronto City FC (14W-6D-4L)	Toronto Italia FC
1965-09-05 24 matches	Montréal Italica (13W-5D-6L)	Toronto Inter Roma FC
1966-08-28 24 matches	Toronto Italia Falcons FC (21W-2D-1L)	Toronto Inter Roma FC

LAST DAY of FINAL (BEST OF 3)	PRESIDENT'S CUP	RUNNERS UP
1961-10-09 Toronto, ON	Montréal Cantalia FC (D W W)	Toronto Italia FC

FINAL MATCH	PRESIDENT'S CUP	RUNNERS UP
1962-08-18 Toronto, ON	Toronto Italia FC won 3-2	Toronto City FC

LAST DAY of FINAL (BEST OF 3)	PRESIDENT'S CUP	RUNNERS UP
1963-09-18 Toronto, ON (2)	Toronto Italia FC (W W)	Montréal Cantalia FC
1964-09-13 Toronto, ON (2)	Toronto City FC (W W)	Toronto Italia FC
1965-09-22 Toronto, ON	Toronto Italia FC (D W W)	Primo Hamilton FC
1966-09-07 Toronto, ON (2)	Toronto Inter Roma FC (W W)	Toronto Italia Falcons

NORTH AMERICAN SOCCER LEAGUE

SOCCER BOWL	NASL CHAMPIONSHIP	RUNNERS UP
1976-08-28 Seattle, WA	Toronto Metros-Croatia SC won 3-0	Minnesota Kicks
1979-09-08 East Rutherford, NJ	Vancouver Whitecaps FC won 2-1	Tampa Bay Rowdies

CANADIAN PROFESSIONAL LEAGUE

FINAL MATCH	CPSL CHAMPIONSHIP	RUNNERS UP
1983-09-11 Edmonton, AB	Edmonton Eagles won 2-0	Hamilton Steelers SC

CANADIAN SOCCER LEAGUE

LAST DAY of SEASON	LEAGUE CHAMPIONS	RUNNERS UP
1987-09-20 20 matches	Calgary Kickers (11W-5D-4L)	Hamilton Steelers SC
1988-09-11 28 matches	Vancouver 86ers (21W-6D-1L)	Hamilton Steelers SC
1989-09-10 26 matches	Vancouver 86ers (18W-6D-2L)	Toronto Blizzard SC
1990-09-09 26 matches	Vancouver 86ers (17W-6D-3L)	Toronto Blizzard SC
1991-09-04 28 matches	Vancouver 86ers (20W-4D-4L)	Toronto Blizzard SC
1992-09-13 20 matches	Vancouver 86ers (11W-3D-6L)	North York Rockets

FINAL MATCH	CSL CHAMPIONSHIP	RUNNERS UP
1987-09-20 Calgary, AB	Calgary Kickers won 2-1	Hamilton Steelers SC
1988-09-25 Burnaby, BC	Vancouver 86ers won 4-1	Hamilton Steelers SC
1989-10-01 Burnaby, BC	Vancouver 86ers won 3-2	Hamilton Steelers SC

CHAMPIONS

1990-10-08	Burnaby, BC	Vancouver 86ers won 6-1	Hamilton Steelers SC
1991-10-06	Burnaby, BC	Vancouver 86ers won 5-3	Toronto Blizzard SC
LAST DAY of FINAL (2 LEGS)		**CHAMPIONSHIP (AGGREGATE)**	**RUNNERS UP**
1992-10-04	Burnaby, BC	Winnipeg Fury SC won series 2-1	Vancouver 86ers

MAJOR LEAGUE SOCCER

LAST DAY of SEASON		**CPL REGULAR SEASON**	**RUNNERS UP**
2017-10-22	34 matches	Toronto FC (20W-9D-5L)	New York City FC
PLAYOFF FINAL		**MLS CUP**	**RUNNERS UP**
2017-12-09	Toronto, ON	Toronto FC won 2-0	Seattle Sounders FC

CANADIAN CHAMPIONSHIP

LAST DAY of ROUND ROBIN		**CHAMPIONSHIP (RESULTS)**	**RUNNERS UP**
2008-07-22	4 matches	Impact de Montréal (L W W D)	Toronto FC
2009-06-18	4 matches	Toronto FC (W W L W)	Vancouver Whitecaps FC
2010-06-02	4 matches	Toronto FC (W W D D)	Vancouver Whitecaps FC
LAST DAY of FINAL (2 LEGS)		**CHAMPIONSHIP (AGGREGATE)**	**RUNNERS UP**
2011-07-02	Toronto, ON	Toronto FC won series 3-2	Vancouver Whitecaps FC
2012-05-23	Toronto, ON	Toronto FC won series 2-1	Vancouver Whitecaps FC
2013-05-29	Vancouver, BC	Impact de Montréal won series 2-2	Vancouver Whitecaps FC
2014-06-04	Montréal, QC	Impact de Montréal won series 2-1	Toronto FC
2015-08-26	Vancouver, BC	Vancouver Whitecaps FC won series 4-2	Impact de Montréal
2016-06-29	Vancouver, BC	Toronto FC won series 2-2	Vancouver Whitecaps FC
2017-06-27	Toronto, ON	Toronto FC won series 3-2	Impact de Montréal
2018-08-15	Toronto, ON	Toronto FC won series 7-4	Vancouver Whitecaps FC
2019-09-25	Toronto, ON	Impact de Montréal 1-1 / won 3-1 on kicks	Toronto FC
FINAL MATCH		**CANADIAN CHAMPIONSHIP**	**RUNNERS UP**
2021-11-21	Montréal, QC	CF Montréal won 1-0	Toronto FC
2022-07-26	Vancouver, BC	Vancouver Whitecaps FC 1-1 / won 5-3 on kicks	Toronto FC
2023-06-07	Vancouver, BC	Vancouver Whitecaps FC won 2-1	CF Montréal

CANADIAN PREMIER LEAGUE

LAST DAY of SEASON		**CPL REGULAR SEASON**	**RUNNERS UP**
2021-11-07	28 matches	Forge FC Hamilton (16W-2D-10L)	Cavalry FC Calgary
2022-10-09	28 matches	Atlético Ottawa (13W-10D-5L)	Forge FC Hamilton
2023-10-07	28 matches	Cavalry FC Calgary (16W-7D-5L)	Forge FC Hamilton
LAST DAY of FINAL (2 LEGS)		**CPL CHAMPIONSHIP**	**RUNNERS UP**
2019-11-02	Calgary, AB	Forge FC Hamilton won series 2-0	Cavalry FC Calgary
FINAL MATCH		**CPL CHAMPIONSHIP**	**RUNNERS UP**
2020-09-19	Charlottetown, PE	Forge FC Hamilton won 2-0	HFX Wanderers FC
2021-12-05	Hamilton, ON	Pacific FC won away 1-0	Forge FC Hamilton
2022-10-30	Ottawa, ON	Forge FC Hamilton won away 2-0	Atlético Ottawa
2023-10-28	Hamilton, ON	Forge FC Hamilton won 2-1 a.e.t.	Cavalry FC Calgary

Books by Up North Productions

SOCCER FOOTBALL BOOKS :
CANADA FROM BRONZE TO GOLD
CHRISTINE SINCLAIR THE G.O.A.T. - 12 FAMOUS MATCHES FOR CANADA
CANADIAN SOCCER'S ALL-TIME TOP 100 WOMEN'S FOOTBALLERS
CANADIAN SOCCER'S ALL-TIME TOP 100 MEN'S FOOTBALLERS
CANADIAN SOCCER'S 2024 MEN'S FOOTBALL ANNUAL

CANADIAN SOCCER HISTORY (SERIES) :
THIS DAY IN CANADIAN SOCCER HISTORY
CANADIAN SOCCER: MEN'S AMATEUR FOOTBALL CHAMPIONS
26 REMARKABLE MOMENTS IN CANADIAN SOCCER HISTORY

HOCKEY BOOKS :
THE WAYNE GRETZKY GOALS RECORD
12 SEASONS: THE CWHL RECORDS BOOK
ANGELA JAMES BOWL SCORING CHAMPIONS
GAME 7 : RECORDS, HEROES & CHAMPIONS
THIS DAY IN CANADIAN HOCKEY HISTORY
WHO'S WHO IN WOMEN'S HOCKEY GUIDE

COLLECTOR BOOKS :
THE O-PEE-CHEE HOCKEY CARD STORY
1979-80 O-PEE-CHEE HOCKEY CARD STORY
THE PARKIES HOCKEY CARD STORY
THE O-PEE-CHEE MASTER CHECKLIST
THE O-PEE-CHEE HOCKEY CARD MASTER CHECKLIST
100 HOCKEY CARD FIRSTS
THE WAYNE GRETZKY COLLECTOR'S HANDBOOK
THE EXPOS BASEBALL CARD MASTER CHECKLIST

COLLECTING THE TOP 100 (SERIES) :
COLLECTING THE TOP 100 O-PEE-CHEE HOCKEY CARDS
COLLECTING THE TOP 100 MONTRÉAL CANADIENS
COLLECTING THE TOP 100 TORONTO MAPLE LEAFS
COLLECTING THE TOP 100 GOALIE HOCKEY CARDS
COLLECTING THE TOP 100 BASEBALL CARDS

www.ingramcontent.com/pod-product-compliance
Lightning Source LLC
Chambersburg PA
CBHW072211070526
44585CB00015B/1284